Stipend Springs' Monetary Murmurings

Securing funding for scholastic success and lifelong earnings.

Peter Xochihua

Table of Contents

1 Chapter 1: Laying the Foundation 5
1.1 Understanding Your Financial Landscape 8
1.2 Budgeting for the Future 11

2 Chapter 2: Scholastic Funding Options 15
2.1 Grants and Scholarships 18
2.2 Student Loans Explained 21
2.3 Work-Study Programs 25

3 Chapter 3: Crafting a Winning Application . . . 29
3.1 The Art of the Essay 32
3.2 Letters of Recommendation 35
3.3 Demonstrating Financial Need 38

4 Chapter 4: Managing Finances in School 43
4.1 Smart Spending Habits 47
4.2 Avoiding Debt Traps 50

5 Chapter 5: Investing in Yourself 55
5.1 Skill Development Courses 58
5.2 Networking for Opportunities 61
5.3 Entrepreneurial Ventures 65

6 Chapter 6: Career Path and Salary Negotiation 69

6.1 Choosing the Right Career 72
6.2 Negotiating Your Worth 75
6.3 Building a Strong Resume 79
6.4 Interview Skills 82
6.5 Professional Development 84

7 Chapter 7: Lifelong Financial Well-being 89

7.1 Long-Term Investing Strategies 92
7.2 Retirement Planning Basics 95
7.3 Protecting Your Assets 98

1 Chapter 1: Laying the Foundation

It all begins with knowing where you stand. Think of your finances like a map; you can't chart a course without knowing your starting point. This means taking a hard look at your current income, expenses, assets, and liabilities. Income is straightforward: It's the money coming in, whether from a part-time job, allowance, or occasional gigs. Expenses are what you're spending. Assets are what you own—savings accounts, investments (if you have any), even that gaming console you could sell. Liabilities are your debts: credit card balances, student loans (if applicable), or money you owe to friends or family. Start by listing everything out in a spreadsheet or even a notebook. Don't underestimate anything, even small expenses like that daily coffee. Those add up!

Understanding your income stream is as simple as adding up all sources of revenue, whether it be from your part time job, help from your family, or income generated from things you sell online, it all matters. Don't forget to calculate how much of your income you are actually getting to keep after taxes, as a rough estimate this number can be between 20% to 30% of your money taken away in deductions that you don't get to use. Calculate your assets, a basic estimate can be all of the money that you own, cash, checking accounts, things of value such as collectibles or precious metals, and things of monetary value. Take your time and make sure that you don't estimate, you must count everything to the smallest detail.

Next, let's discuss expenses. Many people are surprised to find out how much they spend on non-essential things. To gain a comprehensive view of your spending habits, consider tracking your expenses for a month. There are several tools available for this, ranging from simple spreadsheets to more sophisticated budgeting apps. These apps can automatically categorize your spending, giving you a clear picture of where your money is going. Don't skip the small stuff. Those daily lattes and occasional impulse purchases can quickly add up. Once you have a clear understanding of your spending habits, you can identify areas where you can cut back. This could mean reducing your entertainment budget, finding cheaper alternatives for your daily coffee, or negotiating better deals on your subscriptions.

Once you know the amount you have and expenses that you have you are able to track your money and gain an advantage in saving money in the future. Your budget is a dynamic document, you will change it, amend it, and re-do it multiple times per year to keep up with the current situation. You should make a habit of monitoring your spending and adjusting your budget regularly to ensure that it continues to meet your financial goals. Keep yourself on track by rewarding yourself once you meet certain achievements, and don't feel bad if you have some trouble managing the budget at first, it is a learning process.

Now, let's move to the exciting part: Budgeting! This isn't about restriction; it's about empowerment. A budget is simply a plan for how you'll spend your money. There are many budgeting methods, but here's a simple one to start with: the 50/30/20 rule. It is a strategy to split income into three categories, with fifty percent going to needs, thirty percent going to wants, and twenty percent going to savings and debt repayment. This is the most common methodology and is what financial advisors will typically recommend to start with. Needs are the essential expenses required to live. These include housing, utilities, transportation, food, and healthcare. These are non-negotiable expenses that need to be covered to maintain a basic quality of life. It is always recommended to cut down these expenses as much as possible, so as to make room for the next category of expenses. Wants are expenses that improve the quality of life but aren't necessary. These expenses are things like eating at restaurants, subscriptions to entertainment services, non-essential clothing, and luxury items. Reducing the amount spent on "wants" is a great way to save money, as these aren't critical to your survival, but add value to your happiness and quality of life. Savings and debt repayment are important aspects of the 50/30/20 budget. Saving money ensures there is a safety net for unexpected expenses and helps achieve financial goals, like putting money towards a school or even retirement.

Finally, let's discuss setting financial goals. Think about what you want to achieve financially in the short, medium, and long term. Do you want to save for a new laptop, pay off a credit card, or invest in a college fund? Once you have defined your goals, break them down into smaller, more manageable steps. For example, if your goal is to save $1,200 for a new laptop in one year, you will need to save $100 per month. Set realistic and achievable goals that you can track over time. This will help you stay motivated and focused on your financial objectives.

1.1 Understanding Your Financial Landscape

Before even considering scholarships or loans, take a long, hard look at where you currently stand. This isn't about judgment; it's about establishing a baseline, a starting point from which you can build a smarter financial future. Many young adults find this step daunting, and that's okay. It's like looking at a tangled ball of yarn – overwhelming at first, but manageable once you start untangling it. This process is all about gathering information. Think of yourself as a detective, uncovering the clues to your financial mystery. This first step, this financial reconnaissance, will provide the knowledge you need to make informed decisions throughout your scholastic journey and beyond.
First, let's tackle income. For many, this might seem straightforward: what you earn from your part-time job. But dig a little deeper. Do you receive regular allowance or financial support from family? Do you have any side hustles, like selling crafts online or tutoring? These are all income streams, no matter how small. Don't forget things like birthday money or occasional gifts that could be deposited. Once identified, note them all down, including the amount and frequency. Are you getting $50 a month in allowance, or is it sporadic? Knowing how much you can reliably expect is key. If income is less predictable, calculate an average over the last three to six months to get a realistic picture. This is particularly important if you're relying on summer earnings to cover expenses during the school year. I remember one friend who thought they were flush with cash after a summer job, only to realize their biweekly paycheck wasn't enough to cover their needs. By accurately assessing what you're bringing in, you're laying the groundwork for a sound financial plan.
Now, let's confront the inevitable: expenses. This is where many

people stumble because they underestimate how much they're actually spending. The best way to get a handle on this is to track your spending for at least a month. There are countless apps available that can automate this process by linking to your bank accounts and credit cards. However, even a simple spreadsheet or notebook can work. Don't forget to include everything: coffee, entertainment, transportation, and even small purchases. Try to categorize your expenses: housing (if applicable), food, transportation, entertainment, school supplies, personal care, etc. This breakdown will help you identify areas where you might be able to cut back. One common pitfall is underestimating the cost of eating out. A few dollars here and there might not seem like much, but they can add up quickly. Be honest with yourself, avoiding being overly critical. The goal isn't to shame yourself, but to gain awareness. Let's talk assets. These are the things you own that have value. For a young adult, this might include savings accounts, checking accounts, investments (if you've started investing – good for you!), vehicles, or even valuable possessions like electronics or collectibles. List each asset and its current market value. A common misconception is that assets only refer to large items like real estate. Every penny in your savings account counts! Knowing the total value of your assets gives you a sense of your financial security and can be useful when applying for financial aid. It showcases your ability to manage money and potentially contribute to your education.

Next up are liabilities, and these are your debts or obligations. This could include student loans (if you have any already), credit card debt, personal loans, or even unpaid bills. List each liability, the outstanding balance, the interest rate, and the payment schedule. Understanding your debt situation is crucial. High-interest debt, like credit card debt, can quickly spiral out of control if not managed carefully. Student loans, while often necessary for education, are a long-term finan-

cial commitment that needs to be considered when making financial decisions. Having a clear view of your liabilities will help you avoid overborrowing and make informed choices about debt repayment. Facing this part of the landscape can be intimidating, but burying your head in the sand won't make the debt disappear. Addressing it head-on will put you in a much stronger position to manage your finances effectively.
Once you've gathered all this information, it's time to calculate your net worth. This is simply the difference between your assets and your liabilities. A positive net worth means you own more than you owe, while a negative net worth means the opposite. While a negative net worth might seem discouraging, it's not uncommon, especially for young adults who are just starting out and may have student loan debt. The key is to focus on improving your net worth over time by increasing your assets and reducing your liabilities.

Finally, consider your credit score. This three-digit number is a snapshot of your creditworthiness and plays a significant role in many aspects of your life, from getting approved for loans and credit cards to renting an apartment and even landing a job. You can obtain your credit report for free from several websites. Review your report for any errors and dispute any inaccuracies. Building a good credit score takes time and responsible financial behavior, such as paying your bills on time and keeping your credit card balances low. Starting early will give you a significant advantage in the future.

Think of it as financial literacy. Understanding the terms, implications, and importance of it all.

Taking the time to understand your financial landscape is an investment in your future. It provides you with the knowledge and awareness you need to make informed decisions, avoid common financial pitfalls, and achieve your goals. Remember, personal finance is a journey, not a destination. It requires continuous learning, adaptation, and discipline.

1.2 Budgeting for the Future

We must face the facts; budgeting isn't just about pinching pennies; it's a powerful tool to shape your future. It's not some restrictive diet for your money; it's a roadmap, a GPS for your financial journey. As a young adult, you're at a pivotal point, a financial launching pad. The choices you make now, even the seemingly small ones, will ripple through your life, affecting everything from your ability to travel to your retirement age. Embrace the power of proactive financial planning; you're not just saving money, but building the life you dream of. Your financial choices need to be approached with mindfulness. Don't make choices based on short-term wants, but with a future-oriented vision.

The first step in budgeting for the future is to understand your current situation. This involves creating a comprehensive snapshot of your income and expenses. Start with your income. What are your reliable sources of money each month? This might be a part-time job, allowance from parents, or even income from online gigs. Calculate your average monthly income, considering any fluctuations. Now, dive into your expenses. Track every penny you spend for at least a month. Use a budgeting app, a spreadsheet, or even a simple notebook. Categorize your spending: housing (rent, utilities), transportation (bus fare, gas), food (groceries, eating out), entertainment, personal care, and miscellaneous. Be honest with yourself; don't underestimate those "small" daily expenses, like that daily coffee or impulse purchase. Once you have a clear picture of your income and expenses, you can calculate your net income (income minus expenses). Is it positive (surplus), negative (deficit), or balanced? This will tell you where you stand and what adjustments you need to make. Understanding the basics of personal finance is essential for making wise financial decisions.

Once you understand your current financial situation, it's time to set financial goals. These goals will give your budget a purpose and direction. Think about what you want to achieve in the short, medium, and long term. Short-term goals might include saving for a new laptop, paying off credit card debt, or building an emergency fund. Medium-term goals could be saving for a down payment on a car, funding a semester abroad, or investing in a skill development course. Long-term goals might include saving for a house, investing for retirement, or starting a business. Be specific and realistic when setting your goals. Instead of saying "I want to save money," say "I want to save $500 for a new laptop in three months." Break down your goals into smaller, achievable steps. This will make them less daunting and more motivating. Assign a timeline to each goal and estimate how much you need to save each month to reach it. Remember to prioritize your goals. Some goals are more urgent or important than others. Focus on those first. Review your goals regularly and adjust them as needed. Your circumstances and priorities may change over time.

Crafting a budget that aligns with your financial goals is crucial. There are several budgeting methods you can use, such as the 50/30/20 rule, the envelope system, or zero-based budgeting. The 50/30/20 rule allocates 50% of your income to needs (housing, food, transportation), 30% to wants (entertainment, dining out), and 20% to savings and debt repayment. The envelope system involves allocating cash to different spending categories (e.g., groceries, entertainment) and using only that cash for those categories. Zero-based budgeting requires you to allocate every dollar you earn to a specific category, ensuring that your income minus expenses equals zero. Choose the method that best suits your personality and spending habits. Regardless of the method you choose, make sure your budget is realistic and sustainable. Don't deprive yourself of everything you enjoy; find a balance between saving and spending. Track your progress regularly and make adjustments as needed. Use a budgeting app or spreadsheet to monitor your income and expenses. Identify areas where you can cut back on spending and allocate those savings to your goals. Be flexible and adaptable. Life is unpredictable, and your budget may need to change to accommodate unexpected expenses or income fluctuations.

The best budget is useless if you don't stick to it. Developing discipline and sticking to your budget is essential for achieving your financial goals. This requires consistent effort and self-control. Start by creating a budget that is realistic and sustainable. Don't set yourself up for failure by setting unrealistic goals or depriving yourself of everything you enjoy. Automate your savings. Set up automatic transfers from your checking account to your savings account each month. This makes saving effortless and reduces the temptation to spend the money. Avoid impulse purchases. Before making a purchase, ask yourself if you really need it or if it's just a want. Wait 24 hours before buying something you don't need. This will give you time to think about it and decide if it's worth the money. Find free or low-cost alternatives to expensive activities. Instead of going to the movies, have a movie night at home. Instead of eating out, cook a meal with friends. Instead of buying new clothes, shop at thrift stores or swap clothes with friends. Reward yourself for sticking to your budget. Set small, achievable goals and reward yourself when you reach them. This will help you stay motivated and avoid burnout.

Financial literacy doesn't end with budgeting. Building financial literacy is an ongoing process. The more you learn about personal finance, the better equipped you'll be to make informed decisions. Read books, articles, and blogs about personal finance. Follow reputable financial experts on social media. Take online courses or attend workshops on budgeting, investing, and debt management. Discuss financial topics with your friends and family. The more you talk about money, the more comfortable you'll become with it. Seek advice from a financial advisor. A financial advisor can help you create a personalized financial plan and guide you through complex financial decisions. Be wary of get-rich-quick schemes and scams. If something sounds too good to be true, it probably is. Always do your research before investing in anything. Stay informed about changes in the economy and financial markets. This will help you make informed decisions about your money. Financial literacy empowers you to take control of your financial future and achieve your goals.

The future isn't something to be feared, but something to be planned. Budgeting is more than just numbers; it's about empowerment. It's about taking control of your financial destiny and shaping the future you desire. By understanding your financial landscape, setting clear goals, creating a realistic budget, developing discipline, and building financial literacy, you can pave the way for a brighter and more secure future. Remember, every small step you take today brings you closer to achieving your lifelong dreams.

2 Chapter 2: Scholastic Funding Options

Navigating the world of scholastic funding can feel like wandering through a dense forest, but with the right map, you can find your way to the resources you need. Remember, securing financial aid is an investment in your future, and the time and effort you put in now will pay dividends down the road. Let's break down the main funding options available, so you can start plotting your course.

Grants and scholarships are often considered the gold standard of scholastic funding because, unlike loans, they don't need to be repaid. These funds are essentially "free money" awarded based on various criteria, such as academic merit, financial need, specific talents, or affiliation with certain groups or organizations. When exploring grants, don't limit yourself to federal programs like the Pell Grant. States often have their own grant programs with varying eligibility requirements. For example, some states offer grants specifically for students pursuing careers in high-demand fields, such as nursing or education. Then consider scholarships which can be merit-based, awarded to students with exceptional academic records, test scores, or artistic talents. Look for scholarships from colleges and universities, as well as private organizations, corporations, and even local community groups. Websites like

Fastweb, Scholarships.com, and College Board's BigFuture are treasure troves of scholarship opportunities, but it's crucial to filter them carefully and focus on those that align with your profile. Think about your unique qualities and experiences, such as volunteering, leadership roles, or overcoming personal challenges. Many scholarships are specifically designed for students with specific backgrounds or interests. For example, if you're a first-generation college student, there are scholarships tailored to your situation. Or if you're passionate about environmental conservation, look for scholarships offered by environmental organizations. Don't underestimate smaller, local scholarships. While the award amount might be less than a national scholarship, the competition is typically less fierce, increasing your chances of winning. Reach out to local businesses, community organizations, and even your high school guidance counselor to learn about local scholarship opportunities. When applying for grants and scholarships, pay close attention to the eligibility requirements, deadlines, and application instructions. A seemingly minor mistake, such as missing a deadline or failing to include a required document, can disqualify your application. Tailor your application materials to each specific scholarship, highlighting the skills and experiences that make you a strong fit for their criteria.

Student loans are another common way to finance your education, but it's important to approach them with caution and a clear understanding of the terms and conditions. These types of loans allow you to pay education over time. Federal student loans, offered by the U.S. Department of Education, generally come with lower interest rates and more flexible repayment options than private student loans. The most common types of federal student loans are Direct Subsidized Loans, Direct Unsubsidized Loans, and Direct PLUS Loans. Direct Subsidized Loans are available to undergraduate students with financial need, and the government pays the interest on these loans while you're in school and during deferment periods. Direct Unsubsidized Loans are available to both undergraduate and graduate students, regardless of financial need, but you're responsible for paying the interest from the time the loan is disbursed. Direct PLUS Loans are available to graduate students and parents of dependent undergraduate students to help cover education expenses not covered by other financial aid. Private student loans are offered by banks, credit unions, and other private lenders. These loans typically have higher interest rates and less flexible repayment options than federal student loans, but they can be an option if you've exhausted your federal loan eligibility or if you need to borrow more money than federal loans allow. Before taking out any student loans, it's crucial to understand the interest rates, repayment terms, and potential penalties for late payments or default. Interest rates can be fixed or variable, and the repayment terms can range from 10 to 25 years. Use online calculators to estimate your monthly payments and total loan cost based on different interest rates and repayment terms. Consider the long-term implications of your student loan debt and how it will impact your future financial goals. A general rule of thumb is to borrow no more than you expect to earn in your first year after graduation. This will help you manage your loan payments and avoid falling into financial distress.

Work-study programs offer a unique opportunity to earn money while gaining valuable work experience related to your field of study. These programs are typically funded by the federal government and administered by colleges and universities. Work-study jobs are often on-campus positions, such as library assistants, tutors, or administrative support staff. However, some colleges also partner with off-campus employers, such as non-profit organizations or government agencies. Work-study eligibility is based on financial need, and students who are eligible are typically awarded a certain amount of work-study funds each year. You'll earn an hourly wage for the hours you work, and the amount you earn will count towards your educational expenses. The best part is that work-study earnings are often excluded from your Expected Family Contribution (EFC) when you apply for financial aid in subsequent years, which can help you qualify for more aid. Beyond the financial benefits, work-study programs offer valuable career development opportunities. You'll gain practical work experience, develop essential skills, and build professional relationships. Many work-study positions are directly related to your academic field, allowing you to apply what you're learning in the classroom to real-world situations. Work-study can also help you explore different career paths and discover your passions. By working in different departments or organizations, you can gain exposure to various industries and roles, helping you make informed decisions about your future career. Don't view work-study as just a way to earn money. See it as an opportunity to invest in your future by gaining valuable skills and experience that will make you a more competitive job applicant after graduation.

2.1 Grants and Scholarships

Many students believe that a college education is simply out of reach due to financial constraints, but grants and scholarships represent a powerful avenue for accessing higher education without accumulating burdensome debt. These forms of financial aid are essentially "free money" – funds that you don't have to repay. Navigating the world of grants and scholarships can feel overwhelming at first, but understanding the different types available and developing a strategic approach to your search can significantly increase your chances of success. It's like panning for gold; you need to know where to look and how to sift through the material, but the rewards can be substantial.

The first step is understanding the different types of grants and scholarships that exist. Grants are typically need-based, meaning they are awarded based on your family's financial situation. The most well-known grant is the Federal Pell Grant, offered by the U.S. Department of Education. Pell Grants are awarded to undergraduate students with exceptional financial need, and the amount you receive depends on your Expected Family Contribution (EFC), the cost of attendance at your chosen school, and your enrollment status (full-time or part-time). You must complete the Free Application for Federal Student Aid (FAFSA) to be considered for a Pell Grant and other federal student aid programs. But remember, the Pell Grant is just one piece of the puzzle. There are also state grants available, and the eligibility requirements and application deadlines vary by state. Research your state's higher education agency to learn about the grant programs they offer. Public universities and colleges also tend to offer institution-specific grants and some private ones too, so make sure to check the financial aid section of your college's website to see what you might qualify for! I remember feeling incredibly relieved when I received my first grant notification; it felt like a weight had been lifted off my shoulders, knowing that I had secured some funding without having to take out a loan.

Scholarships, on the other hand, can be either need-based or merit-based. Merit-based scholarships are awarded based on academic achievement, athletic ability, artistic talent, or other skills and accomplishments. Some scholarships are highly competitive, attracting thousands of applicants from across the country. Others are more niche, targeting students with specific backgrounds, interests, or career goals. For example, there are scholarships for students pursuing STEM fields, for students from underrepresented minority groups, and for students interested in studying abroad. And then there are the quirky ones, like scholarships for students with a specific last name or for creating a duct tape prom dress. The key to finding these hidden gems is to be creative and persistent in your search. Cast a wide net and explore a variety of scholarship databases and websites. Some popular resources include Sallie Mae, Scholarships.com, Fastweb, and the College Board's BigFuture scholarship search. Don't underestimate the power of local scholarships offered by community organizations, businesses, and religious institutions. These scholarships often have fewer applicants and can be a great way to boost your funding. You'd be surprised what you can find.

The application process for grants and scholarships can be demanding, but it's essential to approach each application with care and attention to detail. Start by carefully reading the eligibility requirements and instructions. Make sure you meet all the criteria before investing your time and effort in an application. Pay close attention to deadlines and submit all required documents on time. A late application is almost always a rejected application. Many scholarship applications require you to write an essay. This is your opportunity to showcase your personality, your accomplishments, and your goals. Write a compelling story that captures the attention of the scholarship committee. Be honest, authentic, and passionate about what you're writing. Proofread your essay carefully to ensure that it is free of grammatical errors and typos. Get feedback from teachers, counselors, or mentors to help you refine your essay and make it as strong as possible. In addition to the essay, you may need to provide transcripts, test scores, letters of recommendation, and other supporting documents. Make sure you gather these materials well in advance of the deadline to avoid any last-minute stress.

Furthermore, don't get discouraged if you don't win every scholarship you apply for. The scholarship process is competitive, and rejection is a normal part of the experience. View each application as a learning opportunity and use the feedback you receive to improve your future applications. Keep track of the scholarships you apply for and the results you receive. This will help you stay organized and identify any areas where you can improve. It's also important to be proactive in your scholarship search. Don't wait for scholarships to come to you; actively seek them out. Network with teachers, counselors, and other students who have successfully secured scholarships. Attend scholarship workshops and information sessions to learn more about the process. Be persistent, be patient, and don't give up. With enough effort, you can significantly reduce your college costs and achieve your educational goals. I've seen friends who initially felt hopeless about affording college end up with enough grant and scholarship money to cover a substantial portion of their tuition. It's a testament to the power of perseverance and a strategic approach. This proactive mindset will benefit you beyond college as well, enabling you to seek out opportunities and advocate for your needs throughout your life.

2.2 Student Loans Explained

Student loans. Just the words can send shivers down your spine. But don't panic! Understanding them is the first step to conquering them. This chapter is your guide to navigating the world of student loans, from application to repayment, ensuring you make informed decisions that support your academic goals and future financial stability. It's not about blindly borrowing; it's about strategically utilizing loans as a tool, one that you control, not the other way around.

Before you even begin filling out applications, pause and consider your options. Grants and scholarships should always be your primary focus. They're essentially free money, requiring no repayment. Exhaust all avenues for these before even contemplating a loan. Think of student loans as a last resort, a strategic supplement to cover the remaining costs after grants, scholarships, and family contributions have been exhausted. Research federal, state, and institutional grants. Talk to your guidance counselor. Scour online databases for scholarships that match your interests, skills, and background. Don't be afraid to apply for even small scholarships; they all add up. Furthermore, remember that work-study programs exist for a reason; see if they can fill a big gap in your needs. By reducing the amount you need to borrow, you minimize future debt and free up your post-graduation income for other priorities.

Now, let's dive into the types of student loans. Generally, they fall into two categories: federal and private. Federal student loans are backed by the government, offering more borrower protections and often lower interest rates. Private student loans, on the other hand, are offered by banks, credit unions, and other financial institutions. They may have higher interest rates and fewer repayment options, so they should be considered only if federal loan options are insufficient. Within federal loans, there are subsidized and unsubsidized options. Subsidized loans, available to students with demonstrated financial need, don't accrue interest while you're in school. Unsubsidized loans, available to all eligible students regardless of need, do accrue interest from the moment they're disbursed. Understanding the difference is crucial because it directly impacts the total amount you'll repay. Also, remember to look at the terms of the loan itself, this will help you in the long run.

The application process for federal student loans starts with the Free Application for Federal Student Aid (FAFSA). This form collects information about your and your family's financial situation to determine your eligibility for federal student aid, including grants, work-study, and loans. Completing the FAFSA is essential, even if you think you might not qualify for need-based aid. Some scholarships and grants require FAFSA completion as part of their application process. The FAFSA opens annually on October 1st for the following academic year, so be sure to apply early to maximize your chances of receiving aid.

Gathering all necessary financial documents beforehand will streamline the application process.

Once you've been approved for a student loan, it's time to understand the terms and conditions. Pay close attention to the interest rate, which is the cost of borrowing money, expressed as a percentage. Understand whether it's a fixed or variable rate. A fixed rate remains the same over the life of the loan, providing predictability. A variable rate, on the other hand, can fluctuate based on market conditions, potentially increasing your monthly payments. Also, know the loan term, which is the length of time you have to repay the loan. A shorter term means higher monthly payments but less interest paid overall. A longer term means lower monthly payments but more interest paid over the life of the loan. Finally, consider the loan fees, which are charges associated with processing the loan. Be sure to factor these fees into your overall borrowing cost.

Repayment options are a critical factor to consider when choosing a student loan. Federal student loans offer several repayment plans, including standard, graduated, extended, and income-driven repayment plans. The standard plan involves fixed monthly payments over a 10-year period. The graduated plan starts with lower payments that gradually increase over time. The extended plan allows you to repay the loan over a longer period, typically up to 25 years, resulting in lower monthly payments but more interest paid overall. Income-driven repayment plans, such as Income-Based Repayment (IBR), Income-Contingent Repayment (ICR), and Pay As You Earn (PAYE), base your monthly payments on your income and family size. These plans can be particularly helpful if you're entering a lower-paying profession or experience a financial hardship after graduation.

Beyond traditional repayment plans, there are also loan forgiveness programs available for certain professions, such as teaching, nursing, and public service. The Public Service Loan Forgiveness (PSLF) program, for example, forgives the remaining balance on your federal student loans after you've made 120 qualifying monthly payments while working full-time for a qualifying public service employer. Be sure to research eligibility requirements and application procedures carefully to determine if you qualify for these programs. Understanding these options before taking out a loan empowers you to plan for your future. Defaulting on a student loan has severe consequences. It can damage your credit score, making it difficult to obtain credit in the future, such as for a car loan or a mortgage. It can also lead to wage garnishment, where a portion of your paycheck is withheld to repay the debt. The government can also seize your tax refunds and Social Security benefits. If you're struggling to make your student loan payments, don't ignore the problem. Contact your loan servicer immediately to discuss your options. They may be able to offer you a temporary forbearance or deferment, which allows you to postpone your payments for a period of time. Alternatively, they may be able to switch you to a more affordable repayment plan.

Finally, I encourage you to empower yourself with knowledge. Use online resources, talk to financial advisors, and attend workshops on student loan management. The more you understand, the better equipped you'll be to make informed decisions and navigate the complexities of student loan repayment. Remember, student loans are an investment in your future, but like any investment, they require careful planning and responsible management. Don't let fear paralyze you; take control and chart a path towards financial well-being. This will make your future brighter.

2.3 Work-Study Programs

Let's explore the realm of work-study programs, a fantastic opportunity to weave together your academic pursuits with practical, paid work experience. These programs aren't just about earning a few extra bucks; they're about building a foundation for your future, developing skills, and making valuable connections, all while tackling the financial burden of education. Think of it as a bridge, skillfully connecting the classroom to the real world, and providing the financial stability you need to thrive in both.

Work-study programs come in two primary flavors: federal and institutional. Federal work-study is funded by the government and offered to students who demonstrate financial need through the Free Application for Federal Student Aid (FAFSA). Institutional work-study, on the other hand, is funded by the college or university itself. The eligibility requirements may vary slightly, but generally, both programs prioritize students with demonstrated financial need. The types of jobs available through work-study programs are incredibly diverse. You might find yourself working in the campus library, assisting a professor with research, tutoring other students, working in an administrative office, or even contributing to a community service project. The possibilities are vast, and often tailored to your interests and skills. The beauty of these programs lies in their flexibility. Your work schedule is designed to accommodate your classes and study time, ensuring that your academics always come first. This built-in understanding and support can be a huge relief, allowing you to focus on your studies without the added stress of juggling a demanding, inflexible job.

Securing a work-study position isn't always automatic, even if you're eligible. The first step is to complete the FAFSA. Make sure you do this well before the deadline to maximize your chances of receiving aid, including work-study. Once you've been awarded work-study, the real work begins – finding a job. Don't just wait for positions to fall into your lap; be proactive. Start by checking your college's job board, which is usually online. These boards are specifically designed for work-study students and often feature a wide range of opportunities. Next, tap into your network. Talk to your professors, academic advisors, and career services staff. They may know of unadvertised positions or be able to connect you with potential employers. Don't underestimate the power of a face-to-face inquiry. Visit departments that interest you and ask if they have any work-study openings. Even if they don't have immediate positions, expressing your interest can put you on their radar for future opportunities. When you find a potential job, treat it like any other application process. Craft a compelling resume highlighting your relevant skills and experience, even if you haven't held a traditional job before. Focus on transferable skills like communication, teamwork, problem-solving, and organization. Write a cover letter expressing your enthusiasm for the position and explaining why you're a good fit. Prepare for the interview. Research the department or organization and understand the job responsibilities. Practice answering common interview questions and be ready to showcase your skills and experience. Most importantly, be professional, enthusiastic, and demonstrate your willingness to learn.

Successfully navigating a work-study job requires a blend of academic commitment and professional responsibility. It starts with effective time management. Balancing classes, studying, work, and personal life can be challenging, so it's crucial to create a realistic schedule and stick to it. Use a planner, calendar app, or whatever system works best for you to keep track of deadlines, appointments, and work hours. Communication is also key. Keep your supervisor informed about your class schedule and any potential conflicts. If you're struggling to balance your workload, don't hesitate to ask for help. Most supervisors are understanding and willing to work with you to find a solution. Treat your work-study job like any other professional position. Arrive on time, dress appropriately, and be prepared to work. Take initiative, be proactive, and don't be afraid to ask questions. Show your supervisor that you're reliable, responsible, and committed to doing your best. Remember, your performance in your work-study job can have a significant impact on your future career prospects. It's an opportunity to build your resume, gain valuable experience, and develop professional skills that employers highly value.

Work-study programs aren't just about earning money; they're about building a brighter future. Think of it as a strategic investment in yourself. Beyond the financial benefits, work-study programs offer a wealth of advantages that can significantly enhance your academic and professional journey. For starters, they provide invaluable work experience. Employers are always on the lookout for candidates with practical skills and real-world experience. A work-study job allows you to develop these skills, whether it's customer service, data entry, research, or project management. You'll also gain experience working in a professional environment, learning how to interact with colleagues, manage your time, and meet deadlines. Work-study programs also offer excellent networking opportunities. You'll have the chance to connect with professors, administrators, and other professionals in your field of interest. These connections can lead to internships, mentorships, and even job offers after graduation. Don't be afraid to network with people you meet through your work-study job. Attend departmental events, introduce yourself to colleagues, and ask for advice. Building relationships is key to career success. Many work-study jobs are directly related to your field of study. This allows you to apply what you're learning in the classroom to real-world situations, deepening your understanding of the subject matter and enhancing your career prospects. For example, if you're studying biology, you might work in a research lab, assisting with experiments and data analysis. If you're studying journalism, you might work for the campus newspaper, writing articles and editing content. By gaining practical experience in your field, you'll be better prepared for your future career. Moreover, work-study can improve your time management and organizational skills. Balancing classes, studying, work, and personal life can be challenging, but it also teaches you how to prioritize tasks, manage your time effectively, and stay organized. These are essential skills for success in both college and your future career. Learning to balance multiple responsibilities will set you apart from your peers and demonstrate your ability to handle pressure and meet deadlines.

In closing, don't underestimate the power of work-study programs. They are more than just a paycheck; they are a stepping stone to financial independence, professional development, and a brighter future. Embrace the opportunities they offer, work hard, and make the most of this valuable experience. Your scholastic journey will thank you, and so will your future self.

3 Chapter 3: Crafting a Winning Application

Many scholarships and grants demand a meticulously crafted application; understanding this truth is half the battle won. I've seen countless bright students falter not because of their academic record, but due to poorly presented applications. This chapter will provide actionable strategies for crafting an application that captures the attention of selection committees, highlighting your strengths and need in a compelling way. Let's dive into the specifics, starting with the cornerstone of most applications: the essay.

The application essay isn't just a formality; it's your chance to speak directly to the decision-makers, to transcend the numbers and paint a vivid picture of who you are, where you've been, and where you aspire to go. Think of it as a personal interview on paper. Start by brainstorming – jot down key experiences, challenges you've overcome, and moments that have shaped your aspirations. Don't shy away from vulnerability; sharing authentic struggles can make your story relatable and powerful. Structure your essay with a clear narrative arc. Begin with an engaging hook that grabs the reader's attention, followed by a well-developed body that explores your chosen themes. Conclude with a strong statement of purpose, reiterating your commitment to your academic goals and how this funding will enable you to achieve them. Furthermore, when editing your essay, look for opportunities to illustrate your points with specific, concrete examples rather than relying on general statements. Instead of saying, "I am a hard worker," describe a time when you persevered through a challenging project, detailing the steps you took and the results you achieved. This makes your claims more credible and memorable. I cannot stress enough the importance of proofreading. Errors in grammar, spelling, and punctuation can undermine your credibility. After carefully editing your own work, ask a trusted friend, teacher, or family member to review it with fresh eyes.

Letters of recommendation carry significant weight; they provide an external validation of your character, skills, and potential. Don't simply ask anyone; be strategic. Select recommenders who know you well and can speak specifically about your abilities and work ethic. Consider teachers who have witnessed your academic performance firsthand, mentors who have guided your personal growth, or employers who can attest to your professional skills. Give your recommenders ample time to write their letters. At least a month's notice is courteous and allows them to craft thoughtful and personalized recommendations. Provide them with all the necessary information, including your resume, transcript, and a brief statement outlining your goals and aspirations. Highlighting specific accomplishments you'd like them to address. In addition to providing information, take the time to meet with each recommender individually. This allows you to discuss your application in detail, answer any questions they may have, and reinforce the key messages you want them to convey. A personal connection can make a significant difference in the quality and impact of their recommendation. After they have submitted their letters, express your gratitude with a thank-you note. Maintaining a positive relationship with your recommenders is not only polite but can also prove beneficial in

the future.
Demonstrating financial need can be a sensitive topic, but it's a crucial aspect of many funding applications. Be honest and transparent about your financial situation. Provide accurate information about your family's income, expenses, and any extenuating circumstances that contribute to your need. Don't embellish your situation or attempt to deceive the selection committee; honesty is always the best policy. Present your financial information in a clear and organized manner. Use tables, charts, or graphs to illustrate your income and expenses, making it easy for the reviewers to understand your financial picture. If you have any unusual or complex financial situations, explain them thoroughly in your application. Include supporting documentation such as tax returns, bank statements, or letters from employers. Highlight any efforts you have made to address your financial challenges. Have you worked part-time jobs, applied for other scholarships, or taken out student loans? Demonstrating your commitment to funding your education can strengthen your application.
In addition to the essay, letters of recommendation, and financial need documentation, pay close attention to the other components of the application. Ensure that you meet all the eligibility requirements, complete all sections accurately, and submit all required materials by the deadline. Proofread your entire application carefully before submitting it. Check for errors in grammar, spelling, and punctuation, and ensure that all information is consistent across the various sections.
Consider the overall presentation of your application. Is it visually appealing and easy to read? Use clear formatting, appropriate fonts, and sufficient white space to enhance readability. Ask a trusted friend or mentor to review your application before you submit it. A fresh pair of eyes can often catch errors or inconsistencies that you may have missed. By paying attention to detail and presenting yourself in a professional

manner, you can increase your chances of making a positive impression on the selection committee. Think of your application as a reflection of yourself.

Following up can sometimes make a difference, but tread carefully. Some organizations explicitly discourage follow-up inquiries, while others welcome them. If the application guidelines permit it, a brief and polite email expressing your continued interest and reaffirming your commitment to your academic goals can be appropriate. However, avoid bombarding the selection committee with repeated inquiries or demanding updates.

Applying for funding is a competitive process, and there's no guarantee of success. But by crafting a compelling application that showcases your strengths, highlights your need, and demonstrates your commitment, you can significantly increase your chances of securing the financial support you need to achieve your academic dreams. Remember, persistence and resilience are key. Don't be discouraged by rejections. Learn from your experiences, refine your approach, and keep applying.

3.1 The Art of the Essay

The essay. It looms large, a formidable gatekeeper standing between you and the scholarship, the grant, the program that could reshape your future. Many young adults view essay writing as a chore, a necessary evil on the path to academic success. But what if you could transform this task into an opportunity to showcase your unique voice, your passions, and your potential? What if you could learn to wield words like a skilled artisan, crafting compelling narratives that resonate with readers and leave a lasting impression? That's precisely what you'll do here, learning to master the art of the essay.

First, before you even begin to type a single word, pause. Think deeply about the prompt. What is the scholarship committee really asking? Are they probing your leadership abilities? Trying to understand your motivations? Uncover your resilience in the face of adversity? Don't just answer the question on the surface; dig beneath it. Read the prompt multiple times, break it down into its component parts, and identify the core themes and keywords. Then, brainstorm. Let your thoughts flow freely, without judgment or self-censorship. Jot down ideas, anecdotes, and personal experiences that relate to the prompt. Don't worry about structure or coherence at this stage; simply capture the raw material that you can later refine into a polished essay. Consider a mind map or bulleted list to organize your thoughts and identify connections between different ideas.

Now, let's craft your narrative. Your essay is not just a collection of facts and achievements; it's a story. It's your story, and it deserves to be told with authenticity, passion, and vulnerability. Think about the elements of a compelling story: a clear protagonist (you!), a central conflict or challenge, a journey of growth and transformation, and a satisfying resolution. Start with a hook. The opening lines of your essay are crucial. They need to grab the reader's attention immediately and make them want to read more. Consider using a vivid anecdote, a thought-provoking question, or a surprising statement to pique their interest. For example, instead of writing "I am a hardworking student with a strong academic record," try something like "The worn-out copy of 'To Kill a Mockingbird' that I found in my grandmother's attic ignited a passion for social justice that continues to burn brightly within me." Be specific and descriptive. Avoid vague generalizations and clichés. Use concrete examples and sensory details to bring your story to life. Show, don't tell. Instead of saying "I am a leader," describe a specific situation where you demonstrated leadership skills and the impact you had on others. Use strong verbs and vivid imagery to create a clear and memorable picture in the reader's mind.

Moving on, let's talk about structure and organization. A well-structured essay is like a well-built house: it has a solid foundation, a clear framework, and a logical flow. Start with a clear thesis statement. This is the central argument or point that you want to make in your essay. It should be concise, specific, and arguable. Place your thesis statement in the introduction, so the reader knows exactly what to expect. Develop your body paragraphs with care. Each paragraph should focus on a single idea or argument that supports your thesis statement. Start with a topic sentence that introduces the main point of the paragraph. Then, provide evidence, examples, and explanations to support your topic sentence. Use transitions to connect your paragraphs smoothly. Transitions are words or phrases that help the reader move from one idea to the next. They create a sense of flow and coherence in your essay. Examples of transitions include "however," "therefore," "in addition," "on the other hand," and "similarly." Finally, craft a compelling conclusion. Your conclusion should not simply summarize what you've already said. It should leave the reader with a lasting impression. Reiterate your thesis statement in a new and insightful way. Connect your essay to a broader theme or issue. Offer a call to action or a thought-provoking question.

Refine and polish your work. Writing is a process of revision and refinement. Once you've completed a first draft of your essay, set it aside for a day or two. Then, come back to it with fresh eyes and a critical mind. Read your essay aloud. This is a great way to catch errors in grammar, punctuation, and sentence structure. It also helps you identify awkward phrasing and areas where your writing could be more clear and concise. Get feedback from others. Ask a teacher, a mentor, or a trusted friend to read your essay and provide honest feedback. Be open to criticism and willing to make changes based on their suggestions. Pay attention to detail. Proofread your essay carefully for any errors in spelling, grammar, and punctuation. Even small errors can detract from the overall impact of your essay. Use a grammar checker or online proofreading tool to help you catch any mistakes you may have missed. Ensure your essay adheres to the specific guidelines provided by the scholarship committee. This includes word count, formatting requirements, and any specific prompts or instructions. Submitting an essay that doesn't meet the guidelines can be an automatic disqualification, regardless of the quality of your writing.

Finally, remember that the essay is not just about securing funding; it's about self-discovery. It's an opportunity to reflect on your experiences, clarify your values, and articulate your aspirations. Embrace the challenge of crafting a compelling narrative that captures the essence of who you are and what you hope to achieve. Let your passion shine through your words, and let your unique voice be heard. The art of the essay is not just about writing well; it's about connecting with your audience on a deeper level and inspiring them to believe in your potential. With careful planning, thoughtful execution, and a willingness to learn and grow, you can master this art and unlock doors to countless opportunities.

3.2 Letters of Recommendation

Securing strong letters of recommendation is a critical step in the funding application process, transforming you from simply another applicant into a compelling individual worthy of investment. Think of these letters as character endorsements, vouching for your potential and highlighting your unique qualities in a way that grades and test scores simply cannot. They offer a crucial third-party perspective, lending credibility to your claims and showcasing your suitability for the scholarship or grant you're pursuing. This chapter will guide you through identifying the right recommenders, approaching them effectively, and providing them with the necessary information to craft impactful letters that significantly strengthen your application.

First and foremost, strategically choosing your recommenders is paramount, far beyond simply asking the teachers you liked most, you need to consider who can speak most powerfully to your strengths and potential. Aim for individuals who know you well, can articulate your abilities with specific examples, and hold positions of authority or respect. A generic letter from a well-known figure is less valuable than a personalized letter from someone who has witnessed your dedication firsthand. Consider teachers who have seen your academic growth, mentors who have guided your personal development, supervisors who have observed your work ethic, or community leaders who have witnessed your contributions. Don't be afraid to think outside the box, perhaps a coach who can attest to your teamwork and leadership skills, or a volunteer coordinator who can speak to your commitment to service. Remember, the most effective recommenders are those who can paint a vivid picture of you as a promising individual, highlighting your unique qualities and potential for success.

Once you've identified potential recommenders, approaching them requires careful consideration and preparation. Don't simply fire off a generic email asking for a letter; instead, request a meeting to discuss your application in person or via video call. This demonstrates your respect for their time and allows you to provide them with the necessary context and information. During the meeting, clearly explain the scholarship or grant you are applying for, its purpose, and the selection criteria. Share your resume, personal statement, and any other relevant materials that will help them understand your goals and achievements. Be prepared to answer their questions and provide them with specific anecdotes or examples that they can use to illustrate your strengths. Most importantly, be upfront about the deadline and ensure they have ample time to write a thoughtful and compelling letter. Remember, a well-informed recommender is a powerful advocate.

Following up is just as important as the initial request, because even the most willing recommenders can get bogged down with other commitments, so it's your responsibility to ensure they have everything they need and stay on track. A week or two before the deadline, send a polite reminder email, thanking them for their willingness to write a letter and reiterating the deadline. Include all the relevant information in the email, such as the link to submit the letter electronically or the address to mail it to, along with any specific instructions from the scholarship provider. If you haven't heard back from them closer to the deadline, don't hesitate to send another gentle reminder, expressing your concern that they might need additional information or assistance. Remember, your goal is to ensure they have every opportunity to submit a strong letter on your behalf, and a timely follow-up demonstrates your professionalism and commitment.

Providing your recommenders with ample resources and insights is critical for their success, because while they know you, they may not know the specific nuances of the scholarship or grant you're applying for. Offer them a comprehensive information packet that includes your resume or CV, a draft of your personal statement or essay, a detailed description of the scholarship or grant, and a list of your accomplishments and activities relevant to the application. Highlight specific qualities or experiences you would like them to emphasize in their letter. For example, if the scholarship values leadership skills, remind them of the times you took initiative in group projects or led a student organization. If the grant focuses on community service, highlight your volunteer work and the impact you made. By providing your recommenders with tailored

information and guidance, you empower them to write letters that are not only compelling but also specifically aligned with the selection criteria, significantly increasing your chances of success.
Demonstrate gratitude, because expressing sincere appreciation for your recommenders' time and effort is essential, regardless of the outcome of your application. A handwritten thank-you note is a personal and thoughtful way to show your gratitude, expressing your sincere appreciation for their support. After you receive a decision on your application, be sure to update them on the outcome, sharing your successes and thanking them again for their contribution. Consider sending a small gift, such as a gift card to a local coffee shop or bookstore, as a token of your appreciation. Maintaining a positive relationship with your recommenders is important not only for future applications but also for your professional development. They can serve as valuable mentors and advisors throughout your academic and career journey, providing guidance, support, and networking opportunities. Remember, building strong relationships with your recommenders is an investment in your future success.

3.3 Demonstrating Financial Need

Demonstrating your genuine financial need is paramount when applying for stipends and scholarships. It's more than just stating that you don't have enough money; it requires a clear, compelling, and meticulously documented presentation of your family's financial circumstances. Remember, scholarship committees receive countless applications, and they need to quickly and easily understand why you deserve their support. This isn't about begging; it's about presenting a professional case, supported by facts and illustrating how a stipend would significantly impact your ability to pursue your education. Don't assume the committee understands your situation; explicitly spell it out. The cornerstone of demonstrating need lies in a comprehensive and accurate representation of your household income and expenses. This begins with meticulously completing the required financial aid forms, such as the FAFSA in the United States, or similar forms in other countries. Pay close attention to detail; any errors or inconsistencies can raise red flags and negatively impact your application. Beyond the forms, consider including a detailed budget that breaks down your family's monthly income from all sources, including wages, salaries, self-employment income, alimony, child support, and any other form of financial assistance. Then, itemize your essential expenses, such as housing, utilities, food, transportation, medical bills, and childcare costs. Be realistic and avoid inflating expenses, as the committee will likely cross-reference your information with standard cost-of-living data for your area. If your family faces unique financial hardships, such as a recent job loss, a serious illness, or a natural disaster, be sure to document these circumstances with supporting evidence, such as medical bills, unemployment notices, or insurance claim documents.

Once you've established your family's financial baseline, it's crucial to articulate the specific impact that a stipend would have on your educational journey. Instead of simply stating that you "need the money," explain how the funds would alleviate specific financial burdens and enable you to focus on your studies. For example, you could explain that a stipend would allow you to reduce the number of hours you work at a part-time job, giving you more time to dedicate to coursework and extracurricular activities. Or, you might describe how the stipend would help you cover the cost of essential textbooks and supplies, ensuring that you have the resources you need to succeed in your classes. Furthermore, consider explaining how the stipend would enable you to pursue unpaid internships or research opportunities that would enhance your skills and career prospects. By connecting the stipend directly to your academic goals and future aspirations, you demonstrate that you are not simply seeking financial assistance, but rather investing in your own potential.

It's crucial to remember that demonstrating financial need isn't solely about presenting numbers; it's also about showcasing your commitment to education and your willingness to overcome financial obstacles. Highlight any academic achievements, extracurricular activities, or volunteer work that demonstrate your dedication and potential. If you have maintained a high GPA while working part-time to support your family, emphasize this accomplishment to illustrate your resilience and work ethic. Similarly, if you have actively sought out scholarships and grants to reduce your reliance on student loans, mention this effort to demonstrate your proactive approach to financing your education. In addition, consider including a personal statement that elaborates on your financial challenges and how they have shaped your character and aspirations. Use this statement to humanize your application and connect with the committee on a personal level, demonstrating that you are not just a statistic, but a motivated and deserving individual with the potential to make a positive impact on the world.

Transparency and honesty are paramount throughout the application process. Avoid exaggerating your financial difficulties or omitting relevant information, as this can damage your credibility and jeopardize your chances of receiving funding. If you are unsure about how to present certain financial information, seek guidance from a financial aid advisor or a trusted mentor. They can provide valuable insights and help you ensure that your application is accurate, complete, and compelling. Furthermore, be sure to proofread your application carefully for any errors or inconsistencies before submitting it. A polished and professional application demonstrates your attention to detail and your

commitment to securing funding for your education.
Finally, don't underestimate the power of persistence. Applying for stipends and scholarships can be a competitive and time-consuming process, but it's important to remain optimistic and persistent. If you are not successful in your initial applications, don't be discouraged. Seek feedback from the scholarship committees or financial aid advisors to identify areas for improvement and refine your application strategy. Continue to explore different funding opportunities and apply for as many stipends and scholarships as possible. Remember, every application is a learning experience, and with dedication and perseverance, you can significantly increase your chances of securing the funding you need to achieve your educational goals and build a brighter future. Consider widening your scholarship searches beyond the well-known national awards to smaller, local organizations that might have less competition. Look into scholarships offered by professional associations related to your intended field of study. These niche scholarships often have fewer applicants and may be a better fit for your specific skills and interests.

4 Chapter 4: Managing Finances in School

Once you've secured the funding to attend school, the next crucial step is mastering the art of managing your finances effectively during your academic journey. This isn't just about surviving paycheck to paycheck (or in this case, stipend to stipend); it's about building a foundation for lifelong financial well-being. Think of it as financial fitness – the habits you develop now will shape your financial health for years to come. Many students stumble here, accruing unnecessary debt and developing unhealthy spending patterns that linger long after graduation. Let's avoid that, shall we?

The first, and perhaps most vital, skill you need to cultivate is the habit of meticulous budgeting. This isn't some restrictive exercise designed to make you miserable; it's a tool that empowers you to understand where your money goes and make conscious choices about how you allocate it. Now, I know what you might be thinking: "Budgeting is boring!" But trust me, having a clear picture of your financial inflows and outflows can be incredibly liberating. Begin by tracking your income – scholarships, grants, part-time jobs, family contributions – and then meticulously document your expenses. Use a budgeting app, a spreadsheet, or even a simple notebook; the method doesn't matter as much as the consistency. Categorize your expenses – rent, utilities, food, transportation, textbooks, entertainment – and be honest with yourself about where your money is actually going. You might be surprised to discover how much you're spending on things you don't truly value. Once you have a clear picture of your spending habits, you can start making adjustments. Identify areas where you can cut back – maybe that daily latte habit can be replaced with home-brewed coffee, or perhaps you can find cheaper textbook options online.

Once you've built a robust budget, it's time to hone those smart spending habits. One of the best ways to do this is to prioritize your needs over your wants. This doesn't mean depriving yourself of all enjoyment, but it does require you to be mindful about your spending choices. Before making a purchase, ask yourself: Is this something I truly need, or is it just something I want? Can I afford this without jeopardizing my budget or going into debt? Are there cheaper alternatives available? Don't feel compelled to always have the newest gadgets or participate in every social event; quality trumps quantity when building lasting friendships and good experiences. Beyond conscious choices, develop frugal habits. Cook your own meals instead of eating out, take advantage of student discounts, utilize free campus resources like the library and gym, and explore free or low-cost entertainment options in your city. Little savings add up significantly over time. For example, opting for generic brands over name brands can shave a significant amount off your grocery bill without sacrificing quality. Shopping around for the best deals on textbooks – comparing prices online and at the campus bookstore – can also save you a considerable sum.

While developing smart spending habits is essential, it's equally important to actively avoid debt traps. Credit cards can be a dangerous tool for students, especially if not used responsibly. The allure of instant gratification can easily lead to overspending and mounting debt, which can haunt you long after graduation. If you do choose to use a credit card, treat it like a debit card – only spend what you can afford to pay back in full each month. Avoid accumulating high-interest debt, as this can quickly spiral out of control. Be wary of predatory lending practices, such as payday loans, which often come with exorbitant interest rates and fees. These loans can trap you in a cycle of debt that's difficult to escape. If you're struggling to make ends meet, explore alternative options such as student loans, grants, or part-time employment. It's always better to seek help than to resort to desperate measures that could worsen your financial situation.

A further point, many students overlook is the importance of building an emergency fund. Life is unpredictable, and unexpected expenses can arise at any time. A medical emergency, car repair, or unexpected travel can quickly derail your budget and leave you scrambling for funds. Having an emergency fund can provide a financial cushion to help you weather these storms without resorting to debt. Aim to save at least three to six months' worth of living expenses in a separate savings account. Start small, even if it's just a few dollars each week, and gradually increase your contributions as you become more financially stable. The peace of mind that comes with knowing you have a financial safety net is invaluable. Furthermore, consider exploring opportunities to increase your income while in school. Part-time jobs, internships, or freelance work can provide extra cash to help you meet your expenses and build your savings. Look for opportunities that align with your skills and interests, and be sure to manage your time effectively to balance work and academics. Don't overcommit yourself, as this can lead to burnout and negatively impact your grades. It's important to prioritize your studies and maintain a healthy balance between your academic, financial, and personal life.

Furthermore, don't be afraid to seek help if you're struggling to manage your finances. Many schools offer financial counseling services to students, providing guidance on budgeting, debt management, and other financial matters. Take advantage of these resources, as they can provide valuable insights and support. Additionally, seek out mentors or role models who can offer advice and guidance on financial decision-making. Learning from the experiences of others can help you avoid common pitfalls and make informed choices about your finances. Managing your finances in school is an ongoing process that requires discipline, commitment, and a willingness to learn. By developing smart spending habits, avoiding debt traps, building an emergency fund, and seeking help when needed, you can set yourself up for financial success both during and after your academic journey. Remember, the habits you develop now will shape your financial future, so invest wisely in your financial well-being.

Finally, remember that money management isn't just about saving; it's also about making informed decisions. Before making any large purchases, research your options and compare prices. Look for deals, discounts, and coupons to save money. Consider buying used textbooks or renting them instead of purchasing them new. Avoid impulse purchases and take the time to consider whether a purchase is truly necessary. Also, understand the terms and conditions of any financial agreements you enter into, such as credit card agreements or loan documents. Be aware of interest rates, fees, and repayment terms. Don't hesitate to ask questions if you don't understand something. Managing your finances in school can be challenging, but it's also an opportunity to develop valuable life skills that will serve you well in the future. By taking control of your finances now, you can set yourself up for a brighter and more secure financial future. Your time in school isn't just about academic growth, it's also a critical period for developing financial literacy and establishing habits that will shape your financial trajectory for years to come. Embrace the challenge, seek out resources, and commit to building a solid financial foundation for yourself.

4.1 Smart Spending Habits

Let's face it, ramen noodles every night isn't exactly living the dream, even if it's cheap. But college – or any form of higher education – doesn't have to bankrupt you. Developing smart spending habits now is like planting a money tree – it might seem small at first, but with the right care, it'll blossom into something significant. This isn't about deprivation; it's about making conscious choices that align with your goals. Think of it as fueling your future.

The first step is to know where your money is going. And I mean really know. Many students believe they're only spending a little on coffee or takeout, but those "little" expenses add up faster than you think. Ditch the mental accounting and embrace tracking. There are amazing free apps readily available that can help you with this. I've personally used a few, and they were incredibly eye-opening. Mint, YNAB (You Need a Budget), and Personal Capital are just a few examples. They link to your bank accounts and credit cards, automatically categorizing your spending. See where you're wasting money. Alternatively, a simple spreadsheet can work just as well, if you prefer a more manual approach. Track every penny for at least a month. You'll be surprised – maybe even a little horrified – by what you discover.

Now, once you have that data, it's time to analyze it. Identify ycur spending patterns. Where are you overspending? Are there areas where you can easily cut back? Differentiate between needs and wants. A new phone might feel like a need, but is it really essential for your studies? Be honest with yourself. This is a judgement-free zone. Maybe you're spending a fortune on entertainment, dining out, or impulse purchases.

The goal is to find areas where you can reduce spending without sacrificing your quality of life entirely. Consider setting realistic limits for each category. Maybe you allow yourself one takeout meal per week, or you find free alternatives for entertainment, like campus events or outdoor activities. It's about striking a balance between enjoying your student life and being financially responsible.

Embrace the art of budgeting. A budget is simply a plan for your money. It tells your money where to go, instead of wondering where it went. There are various budgeting methods, so find one that suits your style. The 50/30/20 rule is a popular starting point: 50% of your income goes towards needs (rent, food, transportation), 30% goes towards wants (entertainment, dining out), and 20% goes towards savings and debt repayment. This rule is not a dogma, it adapts to all needs, be it more savings if you have a bigger income or more needs expenses if you have not much. Experiment with different approaches until you find one that you can consistently follow. Remember, a budget is a living document. It should be reviewed and adjusted regularly to reflect changes in your income, expenses, and goals.

Student discounts are your best friend! Seriously, they are. Businesses often offer discounts to students, so always ask. Carry your student ID and flash it whenever you're making a purchase. You might be surprised at how many places offer discounts on everything from textbooks and software to entertainment and transportation. Take advantage of these opportunities to save money without sacrificing your lifestyle. Furthermore, explore free resources available on campus and in the community. Many universities offer free access to gyms, libraries, and recreational facilities. Local community centers often provide free or low-cost workshops, classes, and events. Utilize these resources to enrich your life without breaking the bank.

Next, cook at home. Eating out is a huge expense, especially when you're constantly grabbing meals on the go. Cooking your own meals is not only healthier but also significantly cheaper. Start by learning a few basic recipes and gradually expand your repertoire. Plan your meals for the week, create a shopping list, and stick to it. Avoid impulse purchases at the grocery store. Buy in bulk when possible, especially for staples like rice, pasta, and beans. Consider joining a food co-op or sharing meals with roommates to save money on groceries. Even simple changes like bringing your own lunch to campus can make a big difference in your overall spending.

Textbooks can be ridiculously expensive. Before rushing to buy new textbooks, explore alternative options. Check if your library has the books you need. Look for used textbooks online or at the campus bookstore. Consider renting textbooks instead of buying them. And don't forget to sell your textbooks back at the end of the semester. You might not get a lot for them, but every little bit helps. E-books can sometimes be cheaper than physical copies, but be sure they're compatible with your devices and reading style. Sharing textbooks with classmates is another way to cut costs, but make sure you have a system in place for coordinating study schedules.

Transportation costs can also add up quickly. If possible, walk, bike, or take public transportation instead of driving. Campus often has transport at disposal, be sure to use it when possible. Look for student discounts on bus or train passes. Consider carpooling with classmates or friends. If you must drive, minimize your expenses by keeping your car well-maintained and driving efficiently. Avoid unnecessary trips and errands. Combining multiple tasks into one outing can save you time and money.

Finally, be wary of credit card debt. Credit cards can be useful for building credit and managing expenses, but they can also be a slippery slope to debt. Only charge what you can afford to pay off in full each month. Avoid carrying a balance, as interest charges can quickly eat into your budget. Look for credit cards with low interest rates and no annual fees. If you're struggling with credit card debt, seek help from a financial advisor or credit counseling agency. Remember, building good credit habits now will benefit you for years to come.

Developing smart spending habits is a journey, not a destination. It requires discipline, self-awareness, and a willingness to make changes. But the rewards are well worth the effort. By taking control of your finances, you'll not only reduce stress and anxiety but also pave the way for a brighter financial future. You are not going to waste money in stupid things.

4.2 Avoiding Debt Traps

Student life, bubbling with newfound independence and exciting possibilities, can also be a breeding ground for debt. The allure of easy credit and the pressure to keep up with peers can lead to financial missteps that haunt you long after graduation. Understanding the common pitfalls and implementing proactive strategies are essential for navigating this period without falling into debilitating debt traps.

Credit cards are often marketed aggressively to college students, offering seemingly harmless perks and rewards. However, these conveniences can quickly turn into financial burdens. The high interest rates associated with credit cards mean that even small unpaid balances can balloon over time, especially if you only make minimum payments. This cycle of debt can be difficult to break, impacting your credit score and future financial opportunities. To avoid this, treat your credit card like a debit card – only spend what you can afford to pay off in full each month. Avoid impulse purchases and keep track of your spending. Compare credit card offers carefully, looking for the lowest interest rates and fees. Consider cards designed for students that may offer additional benefits, but always prioritize responsible spending.

Beyond credit cards, predatory lending practices pose a significant threat to young adults. Payday loans, with their exorbitant interest rates and short repayment periods, can trap borrowers in a vicious cycle of debt. These loans are often marketed as quick solutions for unexpected expenses, but they typically lead to more financial hardship. Similarly, rent-to-own agreements for furniture, electronics, or appliances can seem appealing, but the total cost of ownership is usually significantly higher than purchasing the items outright. Always read the fine print and understand the terms of any loan or agreement before signing. If you're facing a financial emergency, explore alternatives like borrowing from family or friends, seeking assistance from student support services, or negotiating payment plans with creditors. Never resort to predatory lenders who prey on vulnerable individuals.

Student loans, while often necessary for funding higher education, can also become a significant source of debt if not managed carefully. It's vital to borrow only what you need and to understand the terms of your loans. Before taking out student loans, exhaust all other funding options, such as grants, scholarships, and work-study programs. Research different loan types, including federal and private loans, and compare interest rates, repayment options, and fees. Federal student loans generally offer more favorable terms and protections than private loans, such as income-driven repayment plans and deferment options. During your studies, make interest payments on your loans if possible, even if you're not required to. This can help reduce the overall cost of borrowing. Upon graduation, carefully evaluate your repayment options and choose a plan that fits your budget and long-term financial goals.

Another common source of debt for students is lifestyle inflation. As you gain financial independence and start earning money, it's tempting to upgrade your lifestyle to match your perceived status. This could mean moving into a more expensive apartment, buying a newer car, or indulging in frequent entertainment and dining out. While it's important to enjoy your life, be mindful of your spending habits and avoid accumulating debt to maintain a lifestyle you can't afford. Prioritize saving and investing, and delay gratification when possible. Consider cheaper entertainment options, such as going to the park, attending free events, or having potlucks with friends. Set financial goals and track your progress to stay motivated and avoid overspending.

Unexpected expenses can derail even the most carefully crafted budget. Car repairs, medical bills, and other emergencies can quickly deplete your savings and force you to rely on credit. Building an emergency fund is crucial for weathering these financial storms. Aim to save at least three to six months' worth of living expenses in a readily accessible account. Start small and gradually increase your savings over time. Automate your savings by setting up regular transfers from your checking account to your savings account. Treat your emergency fund as a safety net, not a piggy bank, and only use it for genuine emergencies.

Budgeting apps and financial literacy resources can also provide valuable tools for managing your money effectively. Budgeting apps can help you track your spending, identify areas where you can save money, and set financial goals. Many universities offer free financial literacy workshops and counseling services to students. These resources can provide personalized advice and guidance on budgeting, debt management, and investing. Take advantage of these opportunities to improve your financial knowledge and skills.

Finally, remember that seeking help is a sign of strength, not weakness. If you're struggling with debt, don't hesitate to reach out to a financial advisor or credit counselor. These professionals can help you assess your situation, develop a debt management plan, and negotiate with creditors. Many non-profit organizations offer free or low-cost credit counseling services. Addressing your debt problems early can prevent them from spiraling out of control and impacting your future financial well-being. Take control of your finances, make informed decisions, and build a solid foundation for a secure and prosperous future, avoiding the insidious creep of debt that can so easily derail your dreams. You can do this. It's your future, after all.

5 Chapter 5: Investing in Yourself

Investing in yourself is arguably the most crucial investment you'll ever make. Unlike stocks or bonds, the returns on self-investment are immeasurable and compound over a lifetime. This chapter explores concrete ways to cultivate your potential, enhance your marketability, and ultimately, secure a brighter future. We will examine skill development courses, networking strategies, and entrepreneurial pursuits, all designed to empower you to take control of your destiny.

Skill development courses extend far beyond formal education. They represent targeted opportunities to acquire specific competencies that can boost your earning potential and open doors to new career paths. Think beyond traditional classroom settings; the digital age has democratized learning, offering a plethora of online courses, workshops, and certifications. Consider platforms like Coursera, Udemy, and edX, which partner with universities and industry experts to deliver high-quality instruction on a vast range of topics. I, for example, took an online course in data analysis, and that helped me a lot in my job to get a promotion. When selecting a course, align it with your career aspirations and current skill gaps. Identify the skills most valued in your desired field and seek out courses that provide practical, hands-on experience. Don't underestimate the power of soft skills such as communication, leadership, and critical thinking. These are transferable across industries and can significantly enhance your professional effectiveness. Moreover, remember that learning is a continuous process. Embrace a growth mindset and commit to lifelong learning to stay ahead of the curve in an ever-evolving job market. It's not just about accumulating knowledge, but about applying it effectively to solve real-world problems.

Networking, often perceived as a superficial activity, is actually a critical component of career advancement. It's about building genuine relationships with people who can offer guidance, support, and opportunities. Start by attending industry events, conferences, and workshops. Actively participate in discussions, ask thoughtful questions, and exchange contact information with fellow attendees. Don't be afraid to reach out to professionals in your field whom you admire. LinkedIn is an invaluable tool for connecting with individuals and learning about their career paths. Craft a professional profile that highlights your skills, experience, and aspirations. Send personalized connection requests, expressing your interest in their work and requesting an informational interview. Prepare thoughtful questions to ask during the interview, focusing on their career journey, industry insights, and advice for aspiring professionals. Remember that networking is a two-way street. Offer your assistance to others whenever possible, whether it's providing feedback on their work, sharing relevant articles, or connecting them with individuals in your network. Building a strong network takes time and effort, but the rewards are well worth the investment. Don't just collect business cards; cultivate meaningful relationships that can support your personal and professional growth. Remember, the most valuable connections are often those built on mutual respect and shared interests. Networking isn't about what you can get; it's

about what you can give.
Entrepreneurial ventures, even on a small scale, can provide invaluable learning experiences and develop crucial skills that are highly valued in the workplace. Starting your own business, whether it's a freelance service, an online store, or a creative project, teaches you about problem-solving, resource management, and customer relations. Don't be intimidated by the idea of launching a full-fledged company; start small and focus on solving a specific problem or fulfilling a need in your community. Identify your skills and passions, and explore opportunities to monetize them. Utilize online platforms such as Etsy, Shopify, and Fiverr to reach a wider audience and test your business ideas. Develop a business plan that outlines your goals, target market, and marketing strategy. Seek mentorship from experienced entrepreneurs who can provide guidance and support. Be prepared to face challenges and setbacks along the way. Entrepreneurship is not for the faint of heart, but it offers a unique opportunity to learn and grow. The skills you acquire – such as critical thinking, creativity, and resilience – are transferable to any career path. Even if your entrepreneurial venture doesn't become a massive success, the experience will undoubtedly make you a more valuable asset to any employer. Think of it as an investment in your personal and professional development, an opportunity to hone your skills, build your confidence, and expand your network. Remember, failure is not the opposite of success; it's a stepping stone towards it. Embrace the learning process and view every challenge as an opportunity to grow and improve.
Furthermore, actively seek out opportunities to expand your horizons beyond the classroom or workplace. Volunteer for organizations that align with your values, attend workshops and seminars on topics that interest you, and engage in activities that challenge your comfort zone. Travel, if possible, to experience different cultures and broaden your

perspective. Read widely and voraciously to expand your knowledge base and stimulate your creativity. Surround yourself with people who inspire you and challenge you to grow. Remember that investing in yourself is not just about acquiring skills; it's about cultivating your mind, body, and spirit. Take care of your physical health by eating a nutritious diet, exercising regularly, and getting enough sleep. Practice mindfulness and meditation to reduce stress and enhance your focus. Nurture your relationships with family and friends, as they provide a source of support and encouragement. Investing in yourself is a holistic endeavor that encompasses all aspects of your life. It's a lifelong journey of self-discovery and personal growth. The more you invest in yourself, the more valuable you become, both personally and professionally. By prioritizing skill development, networking strategically, and embracing entrepreneurial opportunities, you can unlock your full potential and secure a brighter future for yourself.

5.1 Skill Development Courses

Alright, so you've navigated the tricky waters of securing funding for your education. Congratulations! But getting that money is only the first step. Now you need to invest in yourself to make the most of your academic journey and lay the groundwork for a successful career. Think of it as leveling up your character in a video game – you've got the gear (funding), now it's time to improve your skills. One of the most effective ways to do this is through strategic skill development courses. It's an investment that can yield returns far beyond the initial cost.

Now, when I say "skill development courses," I'm not just talking about formal university classes, even though those can certainly be beneficial. I'm referring to a broader range of educational opportunities that can help you acquire specific skills relevant to your chosen field or career aspirations. These courses can be found online, at community colleges, vocational schools, or even through professional organizations. The key is to identify the skills that are in demand in your industry and then seek out opportunities to develop them. For example, if you're interested in a career in marketing, a course on digital marketing, social media management, or SEO would be incredibly valuable. Or, if you're aspiring to be a software engineer, courses on specific programming languages, data structures, or algorithms will be essential. But how to identify which are the best for you? I believe it's a matter of asking people and reading content about the job titles you want, understanding the tools that they use, and the day-to-day activities of the people.

Before you start impulsively enrolling in every course that catches your eye, take some time to do some research and strategic planning. Ask yourself, "What are my career goals? What skills do I currently possess? What skills are missing that are crucial for me to achieve my goals?" Once you have a clear understanding of your skills gap, you can start looking for courses that will help you bridge that gap. Don't just focus on technical skills, either. Soft skills, such as communication, leadership, teamwork, and problem-solving, are equally important and can be developed through courses and workshops. A lot of students are not aware that there are more than 5000 transferable skills. Some free ways to find courses are by searching on non-profit organizations that offer free courses. Another one is to directly ask instructors if you could attend some classes for free. You never know until you ask them! Also, consider your learning style when choosing a course. Are you a visual learner? Do you prefer hands-on activities? Do you learn best in a group setting? Choose courses that align with your learning preferences to maximize your learning potential.

Okay, so you've identified the skills you want to develop and the types of courses that suit your learning style. Now comes the practical part: finding and selecting the right courses. The internet is your best friend here. Websites like Coursera, edX, and Udemy offer a vast array of courses on various topics, often taught by professors from top universities or industry experts. Look for courses that have positive reviews, a clear curriculum, and a reasonable price. Don't be afraid to shop around and compare different options before making a decision. And speaking of price, don't let the cost of a course deter you from investing in your skills. Many online platforms offer financial aid or scholarships to students who can demonstrate financial need. You can also look for free courses or workshops offered by local libraries, community centers, or professional organizations. The great thing about the Internet is that there is an abundance of resources if you just put the time to find what you are looking for.

Once you've enrolled in a course, it's time to commit to learning and making the most of the opportunity. Set realistic goals for yourself and create a study schedule that fits your lifestyle. Don't try to cram everything in at the last minute. Break down the material into smaller, manageable chunks and dedicate a specific amount of time each day or week to studying. Actively participate in the course by asking questions, engaging in discussions, and completing assignments. Don't be afraid to reach out to the instructor or other students for help if you're struggling with the material. Also, find some study buddies. It helps with accountability and can provide a new view of the things you are struggling to understand. Learning from others is another very powerful tip for any successful student.

Learning doesn't stop when the course ends. In fact, the real learning begins after you've completed the course and started applying your new skills in real-world situations. Look for opportunities to practice your skills in projects, internships, volunteer work, or even personal endeavors. The more you practice, the more confident and proficient you'll become. Keep up with the latest trends and developments in your field by reading industry publications, attending conferences, and networking with professionals. And don't be afraid to continue learning throughout your career. The world is constantly changing, and the skills that are in demand today may not be in demand tomorrow. So, make lifelong learning a priority and always be open to acquiring new skills and knowledge.

Finally, and this is important, showcase your newly acquired skills on your resume, LinkedIn profile, and other professional platforms. Highlight the specific skills you've developed and provide examples of how you've used them in projects or experiences. This will help you stand out from the crowd and demonstrate your value to potential employers. Remember, investing in skill development courses is an investment in yourself and your future. By acquiring in-demand skills, you'll increase your earning potential, expand your career opportunities, and ultimately achieve greater financial success. So, don't hesitate to invest in yourself – it's the best investment you'll ever make. It's not about the money, but what you can achieve with your skills.

5.2 Networking for Opportunities

Networking isn't just small talk at a conference; it's the lifeblood of opportunity, especially when you're trying to level up your education and career prospects. Think of it as planting seeds: each connection you make is a seed, and with proper care, some will blossom into amazing opportunities you never saw coming. You're not just collecting business cards; you're building relationships. These relationships, nurtured over time, can unlock doors to scholarships, internships, job offers, and even mentorship that can profoundly shape your future.

The first step is identifying your goals. What are you hoping to achieve through networking? Are you looking for an internship in a specific field? Are you trying to connect with alumni who can offer career advice? Are you aiming to find a mentor who can guide you? Clearly defining your objectives will help you focus your efforts and target your networking activities. Don't just show up at any event and hope for the best; have a plan! Research relevant organizations, conferences, and industry events. Look for opportunities to connect with people who are working in fields that interest you or who have experience that you admire. Use LinkedIn to find professionals in your desired field and see if you have any mutual connections. Targeted networking is far more effective than casting a wide net.

Consider informational interviews as a powerful networking tool. Reach out to people who are working in roles you aspire to and ask if they'd be willing to spare 30 minutes for a virtual or in-person chat. Prepare thoughtful questions about their career path, their day-to-day responsibilities, and any advice they might have for someone starting out. Informational interviews aren't about asking for a job; they're about learning from experienced professionals and building genuine connections. Remember to express your gratitude after the interview with a thank-you email. This shows respect for their time and keeps you top of mind.

Don't underestimate the power of your existing network. Your friends, family, professors, and even former employers can be valuable connections. Let them know about your goals and aspirations. You never know who they might know or what opportunities they might be aware of. Attend university events, career fairs, and workshops to meet other students, faculty members, and industry representatives. Participate in class discussions and group projects to build relationships with your peers. These connections can become your future colleagues and collaborators.

When you're at a networking event, remember that it's not about handing out as many business cards as possible. Focus on making meaningful connections with a few key people. Approach people with a smile and a friendly greeting. Introduce yourself and ask them about their work or interests. Listen attentively and engage in genuine conversation. Avoid talking about yourself too much; focus on learning about the other person. People are more likely to remember you if you show genuine interest in them.

Online networking is just as important as in-person networking. LinkedIn is a powerful platform for connecting with professionals in your field. Create a professional profile that highlights your skills, experience, and aspirations. Join relevant groups and participate in discussions. Engage with other people's posts and share your own insights. Use LinkedIn to reach out to people you admire and ask for informational interviews. Twitter can also be a valuable networking tool, especially for staying up-to-date on industry trends and connecting with thought leaders. Follow relevant accounts and participate in conversations.

After a networking event, follow up with the people you met. Send them a personalized email or connect with them on LinkedIn. Remind them of your conversation and reiterate your interest in their work or advice. Offer to help them in any way you can. Following up is crucial for solidifying connections and turning them into lasting relationships.

And remember, networking is a two-way street. It's not just about what you can get from others; it's also about what you can offer them. Share your knowledge, skills, and resources with your network. Help others whenever you can. The more you give, the more you'll receive in return.

Also be prepared to put yourself out there. Networking can be intimidating, especially if you're shy or introverted. But the more you practice, the easier it will become. Start by attending small events or joining online communities. Set realistic goals for each networking event, such as meeting two or three new people. Focus on making genuine connections rather than trying to impress everyone. And remember, everyone feels nervous sometimes. The key is to push yourself outside of your comfort zone and take the first step.

Stay consistent and persistent. Networking is an ongoing process, not a one-time event. Keep in touch with your network regularly. Share interesting articles, offer support, and celebrate their successes. Attend industry events and conferences to stay up-to-date on the latest trends and connect with new people. Don't get discouraged if you don't see immediate results. Building strong relationships takes time and effort. But the rewards are well worth it.

Finally, always be professional and respectful in your interactions. Dress appropriately for networking events, and be mindful of your language and behavior. Avoid gossiping or complaining about others. Be punctual for meetings and interviews. And always express your gratitude for people's time and assistance. Your reputation is your most valuable asset, so protect it carefully.

By actively engaging, providing value, and fostering genuine connections, you will not only open doors to funding and career opportunities, but also build a strong support system that will propel you toward lifelong success. Networking isn't just a skill, it's an investment in your future, one that yields returns far beyond your initial expectations. Remember, the connections you make today can shape the opportunities you have tomorrow. Cultivate your network wisely and watch your future flourish.

5.3 Entrepreneurial Ventures

Alright, so you've got this burning idea, a solution to a problem you see every day, or maybe just a passion you want to turn into something real. That's fantastic! This isn't about becoming the next tech billionaire overnight; it's about exploring the world of entrepreneurship, learning valuable skills, and potentially creating something that helps you fund your education and beyond. Forget the pressure of building a massive company, you just need to start small and manageable. Think of it as a learning experience, a way to develop valuable skills, and a potential source of income. The first thing you should consider is your existing skillset, what are you genuinely good at? Are you a talented artist? Do you have a knack for writing? Are you a whiz with computers? Find something that fits your interest and skills.

Next up is to identify problems that could be solved: a common issue faced by students, friends, or even your local community? The best business ideas often stem from addressing a real need. Maybe students struggle to find affordable tutoring, or perhaps there's a lack of convenient transportation options in your area. Try not to over complicate it. It is often better to solve simple problems, than attempting to handle more complex issues with limited resources. For example, If you have a great essay that did well, you could offer to proofread other students' essays for a small fee. If there's a community garden that needs tending to, you could offer your services for a couple of hours each week. These are low-risk ways to learn and earn.

However, a common mistake is diving in without a plan. Before you spend any money or invest a lot of time, create a basic business plan. This doesn't have to be a formal document; a simple outline will do. Start by defining your target market. Who are you trying to reach? Are you targeting college students, local residents, or a specific niche group? Once you have this in mind, try to define the value proposition of your product. Think about how much you're going to charge for your services or products. Do some research to see what others are charging for similar offerings. Don't forget the expenses: what materials do you need? Will you need to advertise? How will you handle payment? And how will your marketing strategy be to catch the attention of a good amount of people?

Now, let's talk about the legal stuff, don't let this scare you off, but it's important to do things right from the start. Depending on the nature of your venture, you may need to obtain a business license or permit. Research the requirements in your area. Also, consider setting up a separate bank account for your business. This will help you keep your personal and business finances separate, making it easier to track income and expenses. Moreover, consider the best way to legally set up your business. Will you be a sole proprietor, a partnership, or something else?

In the realm of online entrepreneurship, consider creating and selling digital products. If you're a skilled graphic designer, you could create and sell templates, logos, or social media graphics. If you're a talented musician, you could compose and sell royalty-free music. Think about ways to package your skills into downloadable products that can be sold online. Remember, the internet offers a vast marketplace with a wide audience reach. A website is not a must have in the beginning. You can use existing platforms, such as social media, to promote your services or products. If you're offering tutoring services, create a profile on online tutoring platforms. If you're selling handmade crafts, consider opening an online store on sites like Etsy or Shopify. These platforms provide built-in marketing tools and customer support, making it easier to manage your business.

One of the most common pitfalls for young entrepreneurs is overspending. It's easy to get caught up in the excitement of starting a business and start spending money on things you don't really need. Resist the urge to buy fancy equipment or rent an expensive office space. Start with the basics and reinvest your profits back into your business as you grow. Also, don't forget to track your expenses. Use a spreadsheet or accounting software to keep track of your income and expenses. This will help you see where your money is going and make informed decisions about how to allocate your resources.

Let's face it: rejection is part of the entrepreneurial journey. Not every idea will be a success, and not every customer will be happy. Learn to view failures as learning opportunities. Analyze what went wrong and use that knowledge to improve your approach. Don't be afraid to ask for feedback from customers, mentors, or other entrepreneurs. Their insights can help you identify areas for improvement and refine your business strategy. And when things get tough, remember why you started in the first place. Keep your goals in mind and don't give up on your dreams.

Do not forget to network, network, network! Attend industry events, join online communities, and connect with other entrepreneurs. You never know where your next opportunity might come from. Networking can lead to valuable partnerships, mentorship opportunities, and even funding opportunities. Also, find a mentor who can guide you through the ups and downs of entrepreneurship. A mentor can provide valuable advice, share their experiences, and help you avoid common pitfalls. Look for someone who has experience in your industry or who has a proven track record of success.

Finally, entrepreneurship is a journey, not a destination. Be prepared to adapt to changing market conditions, embrace new technologies, and continuously learn and grow. The skills you develop as an entrepreneur, such as problem-solving, critical thinking, and communication, will serve you well throughout your life, regardless of whether you continue to pursue entrepreneurship or choose a different path. And remember, even small successes can have a big impact on your finances and your future.

6 Chapter 6: Career Path and Salary Negotiation

The journey from academia to a fulfilling and financially rewarding career can seem daunting. It's easy to feel lost amidst the myriad of options, especially when facing the pressure of securing a stable future. But with a thoughtful approach and a clear understanding of your own strengths and desires, you can navigate this transition with confidence. The first step is honest self-assessment. What truly excites you? What are you naturally good at? Don't just think about potential job titles; consider the kind of work environment where you'd thrive, the types of problems you enjoy solving, and the values you want to uphold in your professional life. Think of past projects that you completed whether you were compensated or not, and try to recall what made you happy about working in them and what was tedious or draining. By looking at your past self, you can gain great insight.

Choosing the right career path isn't about chasing the highest salary or the most prestigious title. It's about finding a field that aligns with your passions, utilizes your strengths, and offers opportunities for growth and fulfillment. Consider shadowing professionals in different fields, attending industry events, or conducting informational interviews to gain firsthand insights into various career paths. Volunteer work and internships are also invaluable. Don't be afraid to experiment and explore different options until you find something that resonates with you. And remember, your career path doesn't have to be linear. You can always pivot and change direction as you learn more about yourself and the world around you. If you want to be extra sure, try consulting with an external expert. They often give great insight as to what would be best for you based on your personal skill sets.

Once you've identified a career path that excites you, it's time to build a strong resume that showcases your skills and experiences. Think of your resume as a marketing tool that highlights your unique value proposition. Start with a compelling summary statement that captures your key strengths and career goals. Then, list your relevant work experience, focusing on accomplishments rather than just responsibilities. Use action verbs to describe your achievements and quantify your results whenever possible. Be sure to tailor your resume to each specific job you apply for, emphasizing the skills and experiences that are most relevant to the position. Proofread your resume carefully to eliminate any typos or grammatical errors. A well-crafted resume is your first impression, and it can make or break your chances of landing an interview. Don't undervalue its worth and be prepared to have several revisions of it.

Mastering interview skills is crucial for securing your dream job. Preparation is key. Research the company thoroughly, understand their mission and values, and be prepared to discuss how your skills and experiences align with their needs. Practice answering common interview questions, such as "Tell me about yourself," "What are your strengths and weaknesses?" and "Why are you interested in this position?" Develop clear and concise answers that highlight your accomplishments and demonstrate your enthusiasm for the role. Dress professionally, arrive on time, and maintain eye contact throughout the interview. Ask thoughtful questions about the company and the role to show your genuine interest. After the interview, send a thank-you note to the interviewer to reiterate your interest and express your appreciation for their time. One of the most common mistakes is for candidates to speak about themselves, which is important, but not as important as the business. Businesses are more interested in what you can do for them than what they can do for you. So when you give them a good reason to want to take you on board, that is when you will have a good chance of scoring the job.

Now, let's talk about salary negotiation, a skill that many young adults find intimidating. Remember, your salary reflects your worth and the value you bring to the company. Research the average salary for similar positions in your industry and location using online resources like Glassdoor and Salary.com. Be prepared to justify your salary expectations based on your skills, experience, and the value you can provide. During the negotiation, be confident and assertive, but also respectful and professional. Start by expressing your enthusiasm for the role and the company. Then, state your desired salary range, explaining why you believe you deserve that compensation. Be prepared to negotiate and make compromises if necessary. Consider factors beyond just the base salary, such as benefits, bonuses, stock options, and opportunities for professional development. Don't be afraid to walk away if the offer doesn't meet your needs or expectations. It's always better to wait for the right opportunity than to settle for a job that undervalues your worth. It's important to remember that not everyone enjoys negotiation, so if you can, try to think about negotiation as another conversation. Don't think about the money as such, instead consider what you are worth and the value you will be able to provide the company with.

Finally, remember that your career journey is a marathon, not a sprint. Continuous professional development is essential for staying relevant and competitive in today's rapidly changing job market. Invest in your skills and knowledge by attending workshops, conferences, and online courses. Seek out mentorship opportunities to learn from experienced professionals in your field. Network with colleagues and industry leaders to build relationships and stay informed about the latest trends. Embrace new technologies and be willing to adapt to changing work environments. By continuously investing in yourself, you can enhance your career prospects and achieve your long-term professional goals. Even a small amount of time dedicated to personal development a day can make a big difference in the long run. Never stop developing yourself because the world won't stop around you. Keep growing and learning so that you will remain competitive.

Embarking on your career journey requires courage, resilience, and a willingness to learn and adapt. By making informed decisions, investing in your skills, and advocating for your worth, you can secure a fulfilling and financially rewarding future. Remember that your career is a personal journey, and it's okay to take detours or change direction along the way. What matters most is that you stay true to your values, pursue your passions, and never stop learning and growing. And always remember to find happiness in your job, and not just money.

6.1 Choosing the Right Career

The world feels vast when you're standing at the precipice of your future, and choosing a career can feel like the most monumental decision you'll ever make. It's not. It's a significant step, yes, but it's also a starting point, one that can evolve and change as you do. The key is to approach it with intention and a healthy dose of self-awareness. I want you to explore, to experiment, and to understand that the "right" career isn't about perfection, it's about alignment with your values, skills, and evolving aspirations.

Start with introspection. What truly excites you? What activities make you lose track of time? Don't think about money or prestige; consider what genuinely sparks your curiosity. Grab a notebook and brainstorm. List your hobbies, interests, and subjects you enjoy studying. Think about the problems you're drawn to solve, the types of people you enjoy being around, and the environments where you feel most productive and energized. Consider your strengths – both hard skills (like coding or writing) and soft skills (like communication and problem-solving). What comes naturally to you? What do people often ask for your help with? Don't be afraid to ask your friends, family, and teachers for their perspective. They might see strengths in you that you haven't recognized yourself. The goal is to create a comprehensive self-portrait that reflects your passions, skills, and values. Only by truly understanding yourself can you make an informed decision about the type of work you want to pursue, not just the paycheck you will receive.

Once you have a clearer picture of yourself, it's time to explore potential career paths. Don't limit yourself to the obvious options. Research different industries and roles that align with your interests and skills. Use online resources like the Bureau of Labor Statistics Occupational Outlook Handbook to learn about job duties, education requirements, salary ranges, and job outlook. Talk to people working in fields that interest you. Reach out to professionals through LinkedIn or your school's alumni network and ask for informational interviews. These conversations can provide invaluable insights into the day-to-day realities of different careers and help you understand what it takes to succeed. Shadowing someone for a day or two is another excellent way to get a firsthand look at a particular job. Consider internships, volunteer work, or part-time jobs in areas that pique your interest. These experiences can provide valuable skills, connections, and a clearer understanding of whether a particular career path is right for you.

As you explore different options, it's essential to consider the long-term implications of your choices. Think about your values and what's important to you in a career. Do you value work-life balance, creativity, social impact, or financial security? How important is it to you to have opportunities for growth and advancement? Some careers may offer high salaries but require long hours and intense pressure, while others may provide more flexibility and personal fulfillment but offer lower pay. There are trade-offs to consider, and it's important to prioritize what matters most to you. Also, think about the future of work. What skills will be in demand in the coming years? What industries are likely to grow? How might new technologies impact different careers? While it's impossible to predict the future with certainty, staying informed about emerging trends can help you make more strategic career decisions.

Next, develop a plan. Once you've identified a few career paths that interest you, it's time to create a roadmap for achieving your goals. This plan should include specific steps you need to take to acquire the necessary education, skills, and experience. If your chosen career requires a specific degree or certification, research different programs and institutions. Consider factors like cost, location, reputation, and curriculum. If you need to develop specific skills, look for online courses, workshops, or volunteer opportunities. Network. Attend industry events, join professional organizations, and connect with people in your field of interest. Building relationships can open doors to opportunities you might not otherwise have access to. Set realistic goals and create a timeline for achieving them. Break down your larger goals into smaller, more manageable steps. This will help you stay motivated and track your progress.

Remember, the career path isn't linear. You may change your mind, encounter unexpected obstacles, or discover new passions along the way. Be open to new experiences and willing to adapt your plans as needed. Embrace failure as a learning opportunity and don't be afraid to pivot if something isn't working. Build a support network of mentors, advisors, and friends who can offer guidance and encouragement. Invest in yourself by continuously learning and developing new skills. The world is constantly changing, and it's essential to stay relevant and adaptable. Finally, trust your gut. Ultimately, the decision of which career path to pursue is yours. Listen to your intuition and choose the path that feels right for you. If you are passionate about what you do, you will be more likely to succeed and find fulfillment in your work.

Choosing a career isn't about finding the perfect job right away; it's about starting a journey of self-discovery and continuous learning. By exploring your interests, developing your skills, and staying open to new opportunities, you can create a career that aligns with your values and provides you with purpose and fulfillment. Your path is uniquely yours, don't let others determine it. This is your life. Make it meaningful, and don't ever stop striving.

6.2 Negotiating Your Worth

Negotiating your worth: it's more than just asking for a bigger number. It's about understanding your value, knowing your market, and confidently articulating why you deserve what you're asking for. For many young adults entering the workforce, this can be one of the most intimidating, yet crucial, skills to master. You've spent years honing your skills, acquiring knowledge, and building experience, and now it's time to make sure you're compensated fairly for all that hard work.

Before you even step foot in a negotiation, do your homework. Research is your strongest weapon. Start by understanding the industry standards for your role and experience level. Websites like Glassdoor, Salary.com, and Payscale offer invaluable insights into average salaries for similar positions in your geographic location. Don't just rely on averages, though. Dive deeper. Consider the specific responsibilities and requirements of the job you're negotiating for. If the position demands specialized skills or experience that go beyond the norm, factor that into your calculations. Think about the company's size, revenue, and overall financial health. A thriving, well-established company will typically have more leeway in compensation than a struggling start-up. Furthermore, consider your own unique contributions. What sets you apart from other candidates? Do you have a proven track record of success in previous roles? Have you acquired certifications or specialized training that makes you a valuable asset? Quantify your accomplishments whenever possible. Instead of saying "I improved customer satisfaction," say "I increased customer satisfaction scores by 15% within six months." These tangible achievements provide concrete evidence of your value and strengthen your negotiating position. This deep dive helps you set a realistic salary expectation. You don't want to aim too low and undersell yourself, but you also don't want to aim so high that you price yourself out of the market.

Beyond salary, remember to consider the entire compensation package. Benefits can significantly impact your overall financial well-being. Health insurance is a big one, and understanding the coverage, premiums, and deductibles is crucial. Retirement plans, such as 401(k)s or pensions, can be incredibly valuable in the long run. Find out if the company offers a matching contribution, which is essentially free money that can boost your retirement savings. Paid time off (PTO), including vacation days, sick leave, and holidays, is another essential element to consider. Don't underestimate the value of a healthy work-life balance. Other potential benefits include life insurance, disability insurance, tuition reimbursement, professional development opportunities, and employee stock options. Some companies may even offer perks like gym memberships, commuter benefits, or on-site childcare. When evaluating the total package, assign a monetary value to each benefit. This will give you a clearer picture of the overall compensation and help you determine if it meets your needs. Don't be afraid to ask questions about any benefits that are unclear. Understanding the fine print is essential to making an informed decision.

Walking into the negotiation with the right mindset is half the battle. Confidence is key, but it's important to strike a balance between assertiveness and professionalism. Remember, you're not an adversary. You're engaging in a collaborative discussion to reach a mutually beneficial agreement. Before the negotiation, rehearse your talking points and anticipate potential objections. Practice articulating your value proposition clearly and concisely. Be prepared to explain why you deserve the compensation you're asking for, backing up your claims with concrete examples and data. During the negotiation, listen carefully to the other party's perspective and try to understand their constraints. This will help you identify areas of flexibility and find creative solutions that meet both your needs. It's also crucial to remain calm and composed, even if the negotiation becomes challenging. Avoid getting emotional or defensive. Instead, focus on presenting your case in a logical and professional manner. Remember, it's okay to say "no" to an offer that doesn't meet your needs. Don't feel pressured to accept something that you're not comfortable with. If the initial offer is too low, counter with a higher number, justifying your request with your research and accomplishments. Be prepared to walk away if necessary. Knowing your bottom line and being willing to decline an unsatisfactory offer demonstrates your self-worth and strengthens your negotiating position.

Navigating the negotiation process also involves understanding the art of compromise. Few negotiations result in one party getting everything they want. Be prepared to make concessions on certain aspects of the compensation package in order to achieve your most important goals. For example, you might be willing to accept a slightly lower salary if the company offers better health insurance or more paid time off. The key is to prioritize your needs and determine what you're willing to trade off. Think about what aspects of the job are most important to you. Is it the salary, the benefits, the work-life balance, or the opportunity for growth? Once you've identified your priorities, you can focus your negotiating efforts on securing those key elements. When making concessions, be sure to ask for something in return. This demonstrates that you're not simply giving in, but rather engaging in a mutually beneficial exchange. For instance, if you're willing to accept a lower starting salary, you could ask for a performance-based bonus or a salary review after six months. Remember, negotiation is a two-way street. Be open to finding creative solutions that address both your needs and the company's constraints.

Finally, always get the agreement in writing. Once you've reached a verbal agreement, be sure to request a written offer letter that outlines all the terms and conditions of your employment, including your salary, benefits, start date, and job responsibilities. Review the offer letter carefully to ensure that it accurately reflects the agreed-upon terms. Don't hesitate to ask for clarification or revisions if anything is unclear or incorrect. Once you're satisfied with the offer letter, sign it and return it to the company. This creates a legally binding agreement that protects your rights and ensures that you receive the compensation and benefits you've negotiated. Keep a copy of the offer letter for your records. It's also a good idea to maintain a record of all communication related to the negotiation process, including emails, phone calls, and meeting notes. This documentation can be helpful if any disputes arise in the future. Remember, negotiating your worth is an ongoing process. As you gain experience and develop new skills, you should periodically re-evaluate your compensation and be prepared to advocate for yourself when appropriate. Your value increases over time, and your compensation should reflect that.

6.3 Building a Strong Resume

Crafting a resume that opens doors is paramount, especially for young adults venturing into the workforce or seeking internships. It's not just a document; it's your first impression, a concise narrative showcasing your potential. A common mistake many make is treating it as a mere list of past experiences. Instead, think of it as a targeted marketing tool, specifically designed to capture the attention of recruiters. Begin by meticulously analyzing the job descriptions for the positions you desire. Understand the key skills, qualifications, and experiences they're seeking. This forms the foundation for tailoring your resume.

The structure is crucial, too. Start with your contact information, ensuring it's clear and professional. Include your full name, phone number, email address, and optionally, a link to your LinkedIn profile if you have one. Avoid using unprofessional email addresses like "coolguy123@example.com." Next, consider a concise summary or objective statement. While objectives were more common in the past, a strong summary can immediately highlight your most relevant skills and experience. Frame it as what you can offer the employer, not just what you're looking for. A summary statement should be a few sentences showcasing your key strengths and career aspirations. Tailor this to each job you apply for, using keywords from the job description. Now, the core of your resume: your experience. For each role, list the company name, your job title, and the dates of employment. However, the real impact comes from the bullet points describing your responsibilities and achievements. Don't simply list tasks; quantify your accomplishments whenever possible. For example, instead of saying "Managed social media accounts," say "Increased social media engagement by 30% in six months through targeted content strategies." Use action verbs to start each bullet point – words like "managed," "developed," "implemented," "led," and "achieved." The key here is to demonstrate the impact you made in each role, showcasing tangible results that resonate with the employer's needs.

The education section is equally important, particularly if you're a student or recent graduate. List your degrees, the institutions you attended, and your graduation dates. Include your GPA if it's above a 3.5. If you have relevant coursework or academic projects, highlight them, especially if they align with the job requirements. For instance, if you're applying for a marketing position and took a course on digital marketing, mention it along with any specific projects you completed. Similarly, if you participated in extracurricular activities or clubs, especially those related to your field, list them. Leadership roles within these organizations are particularly valuable, as they demonstrate teamwork, communication, and organizational skills.

Furthermore, a dedicated skills section is vital. This is where you showcase your technical and soft skills. Technical skills are those specific to your industry or profession, such as programming languages, software proficiency, or data analysis tools. Soft skills, on the other hand, are transferable skills that apply across various roles, such as communication, problem-solving, teamwork, and time management. List both types of skills, but prioritize those that are most relevant to the job. Consider using a combination of hard skills (e.g., Microsoft Excel, Python) and soft skills (e.g., communication, leadership). Tailor this section to each job you apply for, highlighting the skills that align with the job requirements.

Beyond the core sections, consider adding sections for volunteer work, personal projects, or certifications. Volunteer experience demonstrates your commitment to giving back and can highlight valuable skills, such as teamwork and communication. Personal projects, especially those related to your field, showcase your initiative and passion. Certifications validate your expertise in specific areas and can make you a more competitive candidate. It shows that you've taken the initiative to learn and develop your skills beyond your formal education.

Formatting is paramount. Use a clean, professional font like Arial, Calibri, or Times New Roman. Keep the font size consistent and readable, typically around 11 or 12 points. Use clear headings and bullet points to organize the information. White space is your friend; don't cram too much information onto one page. Aim for a one-page resume, especially if you're early in your career. Proofread carefully for any errors in grammar or spelling. Typos can undermine your credibility and demonstrate a lack of attention to detail. Ask a friend, teacher, or career counselor to review your resume as well.

Finally, tailoring your resume to each job application is non-negotiable. A generic resume is unlikely to stand out. Read the job description carefully and identify the key skills and qualifications the employer is seeking. Then, tailor your resume to highlight those specific skills and experiences. Use keywords from the job description throughout your resume. This not only demonstrates that you've read the job description carefully but also helps your resume get past Applicant Tracking Systems (ATS), which are often used by employers to screen resumes. Don't lie or exaggerate, but do emphasize the aspects of your experience that are most relevant to the job. In conclusion, your resume is your ambassador.

6.4 Interview Skills

Alright, let's talk interviews. I know, I know, the thought alone can send shivers down your spine. Sweaty palms, racing heart, the feeling you're about to forget everything you've ever learned – it's all perfectly normal. But trust me, with the right preparation and mindset, you can turn those jitters into confidence and nail that interview. Remember, getting to the interview stage means they already see something they like in you, so this is your chance to show them why they were right.

Firstly, beyond knowing the basics of the company, dig deeper. Don't just read the "About Us" page on their website, that's what everyone does. I always look into their recent press releases, their social media activity, and even news articles mentioning them. Understand their current challenges, their successes, and where they're headed. If you can demonstrate that you've taken the time to really learn about them, you'll stand out from the crowd. Try and find people who work there on LinkedIn too; it helps to know the culture of your potential workplace.

Now, about that dreaded "Tell me about yourself" question. This isn't an invitation to recite your life story from kindergarten onwards! What they really want is a concise summary of your professional journey and how it aligns with the role. Focus on your key skills and experiences, highlighting achievements that are relevant to the job description. Instead of just saying "I'm a hard worker," give them a specific example of a time when your hard work led to a positive outcome. Quantify your achievements whenever possible – numbers speak louder than words. For instance, "I increased sales by 15% in six months by implementing a new social media strategy." Always end this answer by circling back to how you want to make an impact at their company.

Let's consider some common interview questions, and how to tackle them head-on. "Why do you want to work here?" This isn't about needing a job or liking their coffee machine. It's about showing genuine enthusiasm for the company's mission, values, and the specific role. Connect your personal goals and aspirations to the company's objectives. Highlight what excites you about their work and how you can contribute to their success. "What are your strengths and weaknesses?" Everyone knows this one is coming, but it's amazing how many people still stumble over it. When discussing your strengths, choose qualities that are directly relevant to the job and provide specific examples to back them up. As for weaknesses, be honest, but frame them in a positive light. Choose a weakness that you're actively working to improve, and explain how you're addressing it. For example, "I sometimes struggle with delegating tasks, but I'm learning to trust my team and empower them to take on more responsibility." This shows self-awareness and a commitment to growth. Finally, "Where do you see yourself in five years?" This is a chance to showcase your ambition and long-term career goals. Align your aspirations with the company's potential for growth and development. Show them that you're thinking strategically about your future and how their company can help you achieve your goals.

Following up after the interview is crucial. Send a thank-you email within 24 hours expressing your gratitude for the interviewer's time and reiterating your interest in the position. Reiterate a key point or two from the interview that resonated with you, demonstrating that you were engaged and attentive. This simple gesture can make a big difference in leaving a positive lasting impression.

Consider the importance of body language and communication skills. Maintain eye contact, sit up straight, and smile. Project confidence and enthusiasm through your nonverbal cues. Speak clearly and concisely, avoiding jargon or slang. Listen attentively to the interviewer's questions and take a moment to formulate your answers thoughtfully. It's okay to pause and think before speaking – it shows that you're taking the question seriously. If you don't understand something, ask for clarification.

Finally, practice makes perfect. The more you practice answering common interview questions, the more comfortable and confident you'll become. Enlist a friend or family member to conduct mock interviews with you. Record yourself and watch the playback, paying attention to your body language, tone of voice, and overall presentation. Identify areas for improvement and refine your responses accordingly. Remember, every interview is a learning opportunity, regardless of the outcome. Embrace the process, stay positive, and keep honing your skills. You've got this!

6.5 Professional Development

Your journey doesn't conclude the moment you secure that first job post-graduation. In fact, it's merely the overture to a lifetime performance. Professional development, in essence, is about continuously honing your skills, expanding your knowledge, and adapting to the ever-evolving landscape of your chosen field. It's a marathon, not a sprint, and requires commitment and a proactive approach.

Think of your career as a living, breathing entity that needs constant nurturing. Just as a garden requires tending to flourish, your career necessitates continuous cultivation. This means going beyond the basic requirements of your job and actively seeking opportunities to learn and grow. Start with self-assessment, meticulously evaluating your current skillset and identifying areas where you can improve. Don't be afraid to be honest with yourself, acknowledging both your strengths and weaknesses. The aim here is to identify the gap between where you are now and where you aspire to be. This could involve anything from improving your communication skills to mastering a new software program. Take a moment to consider what truly excites you within your field. What aspects spark your curiosity? Pursuing these areas will not only enhance your skillset but also fuel your passion, making the journey of professional development more enjoyable and fulfilling. This self-reflection is crucial for determining the direction of your professional growth and ensuring that you are investing your time and resources wisely.

Mentorship, whether formal or informal, can be a powerful catalyst for professional growth. Seek out individuals who have achieved success in your field or who possess skills that you admire. Don't hesitate to reach out to them, express your interest in learning from them, and ask for guidance. Many professionals are genuinely happy to share their knowledge and experience, providing valuable insights and perspectives that can accelerate your development. A mentor can offer objective feedback, help you navigate challenges, and provide encouragement along the way. Look for someone who is willing to invest time in your growth, listen to your concerns, and offer constructive criticism. The relationship should be built on trust, respect, and open communication. Moreover, don't limit yourself to a single mentor. Cultivating relationships with several individuals, each with different areas of expertise, can provide a more well-rounded perspective. Remember that mentorship is a two-way street. Be proactive in seeking advice, but also be respectful of your mentor's time and willing to reciprocate by offering your own skills and knowledge.

Networking isn't just about collecting business cards; it's about building genuine relationships with people in your industry. Attend industry events, conferences, and workshops. Engage in conversations, ask questions, and actively listen to what others have to say. Online platforms like LinkedIn can also be valuable tools for connecting with professionals in your field. Join relevant groups, participate in discussions, and share your own insights. The key is to be authentic and build connections based on shared interests and mutual respect. Networking can lead to valuable opportunities, such as job leads, collaborations, and mentorships. It can also provide you with a supportive community of like-minded individuals who can offer advice and encouragement. Don't be afraid to put yourself out there and initiate conversations. Remember that everyone starts somewhere, and most people are happy to connect with others who share their passion.

Continual learning is the cornerstone of professional development. The world is constantly changing, and new technologies, trends, and best practices are emerging all the time. It's essential to stay up-to-date in your field by reading industry publications, attending workshops and conferences, and taking online courses. Many online platforms offer a wide range of courses on various topics, allowing you to learn at your own pace and on your own schedule. Consider pursuing certifications or advanced degrees to enhance your skills and knowledge. Don't limit your learning to formal education. Seek out opportunities to learn from your colleagues, attend internal training sessions, and participate in cross-functional projects. The more you learn, the more valuable you become to your organization and the more opportunities you create for yourself. This proactive approach to learning demonstrates your commitment to growth and your ability to adapt to change.

Volunteer work, even seemingly unrelated to your chosen career, presents a surprisingly fertile ground for professional enrichment. It can allow you to hone essential soft skills such as leadership, teamwork, communication, and problem-solving. By stepping outside of your comfort zone and engaging with different communities, you can develop a broader perspective and a greater understanding of the world. It can also be a valuable way to build your network and connect with people from diverse backgrounds. Choose volunteer opportunities that align with your values and interests, as this will make the experience more fulfilling and meaningful. Don't underestimate the power of volunteering to enhance your resume and showcase your commitment to social responsibility.

Embracing failures is integral to this. Don't shy away from challenges or fear making mistakes. Failure is an inevitable part of the learning process. It's how we learn, grow, and become more resilient. When you encounter setbacks, don't dwell on them. Instead, analyze what went wrong, identify the lessons learned, and use those lessons to improve your performance in the future. View failures as opportunities for growth and development. Don't be afraid to experiment and try new things, even if you're not sure you'll succeed. The more you push yourself outside of your comfort zone, the more you'll learn and grow. Moreover, don't be afraid to ask for help when you need it. Seeking guidance from mentors, colleagues, or friends can provide you with valuable insights and support.

Finally, remember that professional development is a journey, not a destination. It requires continuous effort, dedication, and a commitment to lifelong learning. By investing in yourself, you'll not only enhance your career prospects but also enrich your life. It's a way to improve your own performance, and make a difference.

7 Chapter 7: Lifelong Financial Well-being

Imagine yourself years from now. You've navigated college, launched your career, and are starting to accumulate wealth. The choices you make today about your finances will drastically impact that future version of yourself. This chapter is your guide to ensuring that future is financially secure and comfortable. Long-term financial well-being isn't about getting rich quick; it's about building a solid foundation that can withstand the inevitable ups and downs of life, allowing you to pursue your dreams without constant financial worry.

Let's start with long-term investing strategies. Investing isn't just for the wealthy elite. It's a powerful tool available to everyone, and the sooner you start, the better. The magic of compound interest works wonders over time, allowing your investments to grow exponentially. However, blindly throwing money at the stock market is a recipe for disaster. The key is to develop a diversified portfolio. This means spreading your investments across different asset classes, such as stocks, bonds, and real estate. Stocks, representing ownership in companies, typically offer higher potential returns but also come with greater risk. Bonds, essentially loans to governments or corporations, are generally less risky but offer lower returns. Real estate can provide both income and appreciation, but also requires significant capital and management. The specific allocation of your portfolio should depend on your age, risk tolerance, and financial goals. A younger investor with a longer time horizon might be comfortable with a higher allocation to stocks, while an older investor approaching retirement might prefer a more conservative approach with a greater allocation to bonds. Consider using low-cost index funds or exchange-traded funds (ETFs) to easily diversify your portfolio. These funds track a specific market index, providing broad exposure to a large number of companies or bonds, all at a low cost. As you gain more experience and knowledge, you can explore other investment options, such as individual stocks, real estate investment trusts (REITs), or even alternative investments like commodities or cryptocurrencies. However, be sure to do your research and understand the risks involved before investing in anything you don't fully comprehend.

Retirement planning basics are far simpler than most believe. Don't wait until you're nearing retirement age to start thinking about it; the earlier you begin, the less you'll need to save each month to reach your goals. Take advantage of employer-sponsored retirement plans, such as 401(k)s or 403(b)s, especially if your employer offers a matching contribution. This is essentially free money, and you should always aim to contribute enough to receive the full match. Beyond employer-sponsored plans, consider opening an Individual Retirement Account (IRA). There are two main types of IRAs: traditional and Roth. Traditional IRAs offer tax deductions on contributions, but withdrawals in retirement are taxed as income. Roth IRAs, on the other hand, offer no upfront tax deduction, but withdrawals in retirement are tax-free. Which type of IRA is best for you depends on your individual circumstances and expectations about future tax rates. Aim to save at least 15% of your income for retirement. This may seem like a lot, but remember that even small amounts can add up significantly over time. If you can't afford to save that much initially, start with a smaller amount and gradually increase your contributions as your income grows. It is important to estimate how much you will need to live comfortably in retirement. Factors to consider include your expected lifestyle, healthcare costs, and inflation. Use online retirement calculators or consult with a financial advisor to get a more accurate estimate.

Protecting your assets might seem daunting, but there are very simple ways. It's not just about growing your wealth; it's also about safeguarding it from unforeseen circumstances. Insurance is a critical component of asset protection. Health insurance protects you from the potentially devastating costs of medical expenses. Life insurance provides financial security for your loved ones in the event of your death. Disability insurance replaces a portion of your income if you become unable to work due to illness or injury. Homeowner's or renter's insurance protects your property from damage or loss. Liability insurance protects you from financial liability if you are sued for causing harm to others. The specific types and amounts of insurance you need will depend on your individual circumstances, but it's important to have adequate coverage to protect yourself from major financial risks. Estate planning is another important aspect of asset protection. A will allows you to specify how your assets will be distributed after your death. A trust can provide even greater control over your assets and ensure that they are managed according to your wishes. Durable power of attorney allows you to appoint someone to make financial decisions on your behalf if you become incapacitated. Healthcare power of attorney allows you to appoint someone to make healthcare decisions on your behalf if you are unable to do so yourself. Estate planning can be complex, so it's best to consult with an attorney to ensure that your wishes are properly documented.

Finally, be wary of scams. Scammers are constantly developing new ways to defraud people out of their money. Be especially cautious of unsolicited emails, phone calls, or text messages offering investment opportunities or asking for personal information. Never give out your Social Security number, bank account information, or credit card details to anyone you don't trust. Remember, lifelong financial well-being is a journey, not a destination. It requires ongoing effort, discipline, and a willingness to learn and adapt. By following the principles outlined in this chapter, you can build a solid financial foundation that will serve you well throughout your life, allowing you to achieve your goals and live a life of financial security and freedom. Don't be afraid to seek professional advice from a financial advisor if you need help developing a financial plan or making investment decisions. Investing in your financial education is one of the best investments you can make.

7.1 Long-Term Investing Strategies

Let's talk about playing the long game with your money. You've hopefully built a solid foundation by understanding your budget and managing your finances well in school. Now it's time to think about how to make your money work for you over the long haul. This is where long-term investing strategies come into play, and it's crucial for securing your financial future.

Think of investing as planting a tree. You don't expect to get fruit the next day. You need to nurture it, protect it, and give it time to grow. The same goes for your investments. Patience and a long-term mindset are key to success. Don't get caught up in the short-term ups and downs of the market. Instead, focus on the bigger picture and the potential for long-term growth.

So, where do you even begin? Let's start with understanding different investment options. Stocks, bonds, and mutual funds are the most common, but there are others too. Stocks represent ownership in a company, and their value can fluctuate significantly. They offer the potential for high returns, but they also come with higher risk. Bonds, on the other hand, are essentially loans you make to a company or government. They are generally considered less risky than stocks, but they also offer lower returns. Mutual funds are a collection of stocks, bonds, or other assets managed by a professional fund manager. They offer diversification and can be a good option for beginners. Beyond these, you might consider real estate, which involves purchasing property with the aim of generating income or capital appreciation. The returns from real estate can be substantial but it can also be quite illiquid. Consider commodities like gold or silver as well, but do so with caution, as they can be highly speculative.

The next step is figuring out your risk tolerance. Are you comfortable with the possibility of losing some money in exchange for potentially higher returns, or do you prefer to play it safe? This will help you determine the right mix of investments for your portfolio. A younger investor with a longer time horizon can typically afford to take on more risk than an older investor who is closer to retirement. Take online risk assessment quizzes. These questionnaires assess your comfort level with market volatility and help you understand the kind of losses you are willing to endure in exchange for potential gains. Understanding your risk tolerance also requires introspection. Ask yourself how you would react to a significant market downturn. Would you panic and sell your investments, or would you stay the course and ride it out?

Diversification is the cornerstone of any good long-term investing strategy. Don't put all your eggs in one basket. By spreading your investments across different asset classes, industries, and geographic regions, you can reduce your overall risk. For example, you might invest in a mix of stocks, bonds, and real estate. Within your stock portfolio, you might invest in companies of different sizes and in different sectors, such as technology, healthcare, and consumer goods. Consider international diversification. Invest in companies located in different countries to protect your portfolio from economic downturns in your local market.

Dollar-cost averaging is a simple yet powerful strategy that can help you build wealth over time. It involves investing a fixed amount of money at regular intervals, regardless of the market conditions. This means that you'll buy more shares when prices are low and fewer shares when prices are high. Over time, this can help you reduce your average cost per share and increase your overall returns. Set up an automatic investment plan. Many brokerage firms allow you to automatically transfer money from your bank account to your investment account and invest it in your chosen assets on a regular basis.

Rebalancing your portfolio is another important aspect of long-term investing. Over time, your investments will grow at different rates, which can throw your portfolio out of balance. For example, if stocks perform well, they might become a larger percentage of your portfolio than you originally intended. Rebalancing involves selling some of your winning investments and buying more of your losing investments to bring your portfolio back to its original allocation. This helps you maintain your desired level of risk and stay on track to achieve your financial goals. Review your portfolio at least once a year. As your financial goals change, your portfolio allocation may also need to be adjusted.

Don't try to time the market. It's nearly impossible to predict when the market will go up or down. Instead of trying to time the market, focus on investing consistently over the long term. Remember, it's about time in the market, not timing the market.

Be mindful of fees. Investment fees can eat into your returns over time.

Choose low-cost investment options, such as index funds or exchange-traded funds (ETFs). These funds typically have lower expense ratios than actively managed funds. Look for hidden fees. Some investment firms charge hidden fees for things like account maintenance, transactions, or advice.
Don't be afraid to seek professional advice. A financial advisor can help you create a personalized investment plan based on your individual circumstances and goals. They can also provide guidance on choosing the right investments and managing your portfolio. Look for a fee-only advisor. Fee-only advisors are compensated solely by the fees they charge their clients, which means they have no incentive to recommend products that are not in your best interest.
The most important thing is to start early and be consistent. The sooner you start investing, the more time your money has to grow. Even small amounts can make a big difference over time. So, don't wait until you have a lot of money to start investing. Start with what you can afford and gradually increase your contributions as your income grows. Consider setting up a Roth IRA as soon as you are eligible. These accounts can offer tax-advantaged growth.
Long-term investing is a marathon, not a sprint. It takes time, patience, and discipline to build wealth. But with a well-thought-out strategy and a commitment to staying the course, you can achieve your financial goals and secure your future.

7.2 Retirement Planning Basics

Retirement might seem a lifetime away when you're juggling classes, social life, and the immediate financial demands of being a young adult. However, the power of compound interest and the long runway you have at your age makes understanding retirement planning basics now incredibly beneficial. Ignoring this aspect of personal finance can severely hinder your future financial security. Let's debunk some common myths and map out the fundamentals.

The first thing you need to wrap your head around is that retirement is expensive. Seriously expensive. Many people underestimate the costs involved in maintaining their desired lifestyle, including healthcare, housing, and leisure activities, once they stop working. Future inflation is hard to predict but it is worth taking into consideration. You need to understand the importance of starting early, I know it sounds boring, but it could change your life. The earlier you start saving, the more time your money has to grow through the magic of compound interest. Even small, consistent contributions can make a massive difference over several decades. Don't fall into the trap of thinking you'll catch up later. Life has a funny way of throwing unexpected expenses your way, and it's far better to have a head start.

Let's talk about retirement accounts. You'll encounter various types, each with its own set of rules and benefits. A crucial decision revolves around choosing between traditional and Roth accounts. Traditional accounts offer tax deductions on contributions now, but you'll pay taxes on withdrawals in retirement. Roth accounts, on the other hand, don't provide an upfront tax deduction, but withdrawals in retirement are tax-free. Consider your current and projected future tax brackets when making this decision. If you anticipate being in a higher tax bracket later in life, a Roth account might be more advantageous. Also, remember that you might be able to start from 0.

Now, let's dive into investment strategies. Diversification is your best friend. Don't put all your eggs in one basket. Spread your investments across various asset classes, such as stocks, bonds, and real estate. Stocks generally offer higher potential returns but also come with greater risk. Bonds are typically more stable but provide lower returns.

The ideal asset allocation depends on your risk tolerance and time horizon. As a young adult, you likely have a longer time horizon, which allows you to take on more risk in pursuit of higher returns. Also, don't get caught up in chasing hot stocks or get-rich-quick schemes. Investing is a long-term game, and patience is key.

Another thing to keep in mind is fees. Fees can eat into your returns over time. Pay attention to expense ratios and other fees associated with your investment accounts. Opt for low-cost index funds or exchange-traded funds (ETFs) to minimize these costs. Every dollar saved on fees is a dollar that can compound and grow your retirement savings. Don't underestimate the impact of seemingly small fees over the long term. They can significantly reduce your overall returns. Also, consider seeking advice from a qualified financial advisor. They can help you create a personalized retirement plan tailored to your specific circumstances and goals.

Do not forget to factor in inflation. Inflation erodes the purchasing power of your money over time. What costs $1 today might cost significantly more in the future. Ensure your retirement savings are growing at a rate that outpaces inflation. Historically, stocks have provided a better hedge against inflation than bonds or cash. Regularly review and adjust your investment portfolio to account for changing inflation rates and economic conditions. Ignoring inflation can leave you with insufficient funds to cover your expenses in retirement.

Rebalancing your portfolio is important. Over time, your initial asset allocation will likely drift as different investments perform differently. Rebalancing involves selling some investments that have performed well and buying others that have underperformed to restore your desired asset allocation. This helps you maintain your risk tolerance and stay on track towards your retirement goals. Rebalancing is not about timing the market; it's about maintaining a disciplined investment strat-

egy.
And lastly, remember that retirement planning is not a one-time event; it's an ongoing process. Regularly review and adjust your plan as your circumstances change. Life events such as marriage, children, job changes, and unexpected expenses can all impact your retirement savings. Stay informed, stay disciplined, and don't be afraid to seek professional guidance when needed. Your future self will thank you for it. Your dedication to saving and planning early will contribute to long-term wealth. Keep learning, keep growing, and keep investing in your future, so you can look forward to a comfortable and fulfilling retirement.
You have to plan for healthcare costs. Healthcare expenses tend to increase as you age. Factor in these costs when estimating your retirement needs. Consider purchasing long-term care insurance to protect yourself from the potentially devastating costs of long-term care. Explore options for healthcare coverage in retirement, such as Medicare and supplemental insurance plans.

7.3 Protecting Your Assets

Alright, let's talk about keeping what's yours safe. You've worked hard to secure funding for your education, managed your money wisely, and maybe even started investing. Now, it's crucial to protect those assets from potential threats. This isn't about being paranoid; it's about being smart and proactive. Think of it like this: you wouldn't leave your bike unlocked in a busy city, would you? Protecting your assets is similar – it involves taking sensible precautions to minimize risk.
Insurance is your first line of defense. For young adults, this often starts with understanding your parents' insurance policies. Are you still covered under their health insurance? What about their auto insurance if

you drive their car? Understanding these coverages is crucial. As you gain independence, you'll need to acquire your own insurance policies. Health insurance is non-negotiable. A single unexpected medical bill can wipe out your savings. Explore different options like student health plans, plans offered through your employer (once you're working), or the Affordable Care Act marketplace. Renters insurance is another essential. It protects your belongings in your apartment or dorm from theft, fire, or other covered events. It's surprisingly affordable and can save you a lot of heartache and financial burden if something goes wrong. Think about it – replacing all your electronics, clothes, and furniture would be incredibly expensive without insurance. Auto insurance is mandatory if you own a car, and the type of coverage you need depends on your state laws and your individual circumstances. Liability insurance is the minimum, but you might also want to consider collision and comprehensive coverage to protect your car from accidents and other damage. Disability insurance is something to consider as you progress in your career. It provides income if you become unable to work due to illness or injury. While it might seem unnecessary when you're young and healthy, it's a valuable safety net to protect your earning potential.

Beyond insurance, estate planning is another crucial aspect of asset protection. I know, I know, it sounds like something for older people with vast estates. But even young adults need a basic estate plan. At a minimum, this includes a will. A will specifies how you want your assets distributed after your death. Even if you don't have significant assets, a will can ensure that your belongings go to the people you care about. It also allows you to name a guardian for any minor children you might have. A durable power of attorney is another important document. This allows you to appoint someone to make financial decisions on your behalf if you become incapacitated. This could be a parent, a sibling, or a trusted friend. Without a power of attorney, your loved ones might have to go to court to get the authority to manage your finances, which can be time-consuming and expensive. A healthcare proxy, also known as a medical power of attorney, allows you to appoint someone to make healthcare decisions on your behalf if you are unable to do so yourself. This is especially important if you have strong preferences about medical treatment. These documents, while seemingly morbid, ensure your wishes are respected and your affairs are handled according to your desires, even if you can't express them yourself.

Protecting your digital assets is just as important as protecting your physical assets. In today's world, much of our lives are online. That means our bank accounts, social media profiles, and personal information are vulnerable to hackers and identity thieves. Start by using strong, unique passwords for all your online accounts. A password manager can help you create and store complex passwords without having to memorize them. Enable two-factor authentication (2FA) whenever possible. This adds an extra layer of security by requiring a code from your phone or email in addition to your password. Be wary of phishing emails and scams. Never click on links or open attachments from unknown senders. Always double-check the sender's email address to make sure it's legitimate. Monitor your credit report regularly. You can get a free copy of your credit report from each of the three major credit bureaus (Equifax, Experian, and TransUnion) once a year. Review your report for any signs of fraud or identity theft, such as unauthorized accounts or inquiries. Consider freezing your credit. This prevents anyone from opening new accounts in your name. It's a simple and effective way to protect yourself from identity theft.

Finally, stay informed about financial scams and fraud. Scammers are constantly coming up with new ways to steal your money. Be skeptical of unsolicited offers, especially those that seem too good to be true.

Never give out your personal information, such as your Social Security number or bank account details, to anyone you don't trust. If you're unsure about an offer, do your research or consult with a trusted financial advisor. By staying informed and vigilant, you can protect yourself from becoming a victim of fraud. Remember, protecting your assets is an ongoing process. It requires you to be proactive, informed, and diligent. But the peace of mind it provides is well worth the effort. You've worked hard to build your financial foundation; now, take the necessary steps to protect it.

www.ingramcontent.com/pod-product-compliance
Lightning Source LLC
LaVergne TN
LVHW022013200926
848481LV00007B/2370

* 9 7 9 8 8 6 9 0 3 6 7 3 5 *